Call Me Zach Hively

Also by Zach Hively

Owl Poems
Desert Apocrypha
Wild Expectations (with Magdalena Lily McCarson)

Call Me
Zach Hively
Because That
Is My Name

essays

Casa Urraca Press
A B I Q U I Ú

Cover design by Hayley Kirkman.
Author photograph by Magdalena Lily McCarson.
Set in Meno and Runda.

First edition

27 26 25   2 3 4 5 6 7

ISBN 978-1-956375-07-7
Ebook ISBN 978-1-956375-23-7

CASA URRACA PRESS

an imprint of Casa Urraca, Ltd.
casaurracapress.com

For Uncle Bob,
because I sure didn't get this from my parents.

Contents

The Introduction

WRITING A BOOK IS SUPPOSED TO BE a crowning achievement in a writer's life. One must spend years, sometimes entire months, in deep contemplation, self-reflection, and total isolation in order to tease out the meaningful contributions to one's life that brought one to the brink of a lifetime of royalty checks. Then, one must actually write the book.

But in my experience, the challenge of writing a book is mere marshmallow fluff compared to the heavy lifting of crafting the perfect introduction.

The Introduction is where the skillful author introduces the Unifying Themes and Greater Purposes that Oprah will later discuss with him as part of her presidential campaign tour. Within these few pages, the author draws out the greater work's key concepts by using an illustrative metaphor or some other spare literary device, so that book groups can truncate their discussions and go straight to drinking wine.

The trick for the author, of course, is to decide which illustrative metaphor he's going to use, because he already put most of his good stories inside the book itself and, really, does the world need one more story about me evading encounters with bears?

Of course it does! But I don't want to blow my bear-wad up front. So instead, I'm writing the Introduction about a Life Decision that really fails to put those bear encounters in perspective.

It begins, as many stories do, with the words "If my dad can ride his bike over those mountains, then it can't be *that* hard."

I had just moved to Durango, Colorado, to live off my leftover student loans. You would not recognize me then. You also would not recognize me now, unless we have met before. But I was a different person before saddling up for the Iron Horse Bicycle Classic, a typically Coloradan rite of passage. I had long been a dedicated indoorsman. As activities go, a weekly Uno night was more my cup of tea. Hell, cups of tea were my cup of tea.

The annual Iron Horse ride covers the fifty-mile stretch of highway between the mining and railroad towns of Durango and Silverton, while scaling a pair of ten-thousand-foot mountain passes. I had mounted a bicycle exactly twice since I was eight years old, and put the bike in actual motion only one of those times. But my dear father had participated in the Iron Horse ride for years, despite being, biologically speaking, old. And if Pops could do it, then so could I.

I called him up and shared my resolution. He said, "You're still young, dude. I think if you really put your mind to it, you can manage it. Definitely. Absolutely. No, really."

He tried to warn me about the little things, though. Things like sitting in the saddle for hours. Puh-*leeze*! I was a veteran sitter. Sitting is the best way to read books and drink tea. Plus, all the bicycling exertion meant I needed fuel. I could eat anything I wanted, whenever I wanted. And I was already good at eating, too.

Pretty soon, I extended my training to include leaving the house—on my bike!—for actual training rides. And, though it pains me now to admit it, I proved that you *can* forget how to ride a bicycle.

But I had an entry fee and paternal pride on the line. I had to accomplish this feat to disprove all the people who say millennials are lazy, worthless bums destroying America, even though I'm not sure what a millennial is, exactly, or if I am one. Besides, the experience of training for the ride might provide fodder for a future Introduction. So by gum, I rode my bike. I rode it even though I was not a genetically-endowed cyclist with sponsored clothing. I rode it even though my blood was not made of energy gel. I rode it even though it meant consuming protein bars with experimental seasonal flavors like "gingerbread" and "adventure."

I rode it even though I had to shelve my self-respect and take the plunge, literally, into Spandex.

If clothing makes the man, then what's it say when my clothing requires lubricant? Bike shorts come with these baboon-blue butt pads that are supposed to cushion your tush, except they don't do so very effectively because you still have to smear cold cream around your crotch before heading out for a sub-freezing January training ride.

But that shock was not the true hardship of my two-wheeled endeavor. No, that was the masochistic moment known as the "graduated stress test."

With Chamois Butt'r spread on my biscuits, I faced my local neighborhood nemesis—a hill with seven hundred vertical feet of climb compressed into two miles of pavement—to isolate my maximum heart rate. Pops said this test was a key element of an efficient training regimen. I strapped on a chest device that talks to my bike computer, warmed up, then raced toward the Nemesis with everything I had. When I had nothing left, I disintegrated to my base elements, like a pile of bear scat on the side of the road or a seasonally flavored protein bar. And being at that moment legally dead, I missed reading the numbers on the computer screen that revealed my maximum heart rate.

I don't know why this experience was a key element of an efficient training regimen, exactly, other than it gave me another way to build sympathy for my character in this Introduction. It also showed Pops that I was serious about my training. And as we all know, future-President Oprah's readers are suckers for a good father-son bonding story.

As I kept riding, I earned a fresh perspective on my new Colorado home from the seat of my thickening bum calluses. I discovered that bicycling isn't really about the chain grease or the space-age food. It's about communing with our wider environment. It's about making sure I beat Pops across the finish line. And it's about finalizing my growth as a human being by the time I was twenty-seven years old.

On the day of the Iron Horse, when I careened down the last mountain into Silverton, I emerged from the cocoon of early life and young adulthood into this blazing mega-butterfly you read today. No more youthful insecurities. No more "living and learning" or "emotional development." If I could conquer mountains, then I was basically an expert on life.

I wrote my first installment for what became my *Fool's Gold* column in order to commemorate the day of my metamorphosis. I soon branched out from bicycling to tackle the defining topics of our day, topics that required a specialized brand of maturity, insight, and a really poor sense of smell: gender and masculinity in the modern era, family holidays, other people's dogs, finding friendship as a hermit who dislikes people, and so on and so forth.

This book is the collected wisdom of a guy who has got it all figured out. Who sees things exactly as they are. And who has decided, in direct contradiction of capitalism, to share it all via the written word.

For the past ten years, both of my readers had to wait weeks, sometimes even days, for my next *Fool's Gold* column. Now, there is no more waiting. This collection of essays buckles you into my sidecar so you can ride through several years of my life with me—well into my mid-thirties, in fact, which is the age at which you can scoff at yourself for thinking you knew *anything* at twenty-seven. (I am now nearly forty, and I am starting to scoff at what I thought I knew at thirty-five. Will this never end?) In this book, I open my home to friends, apply to be a festival queen, shop for marijuana, and travel to St. Louis so you don't have to. You can flip this book open to read any piece you like, in any order you like. Or you can read it straight through to appreciate the subtle nuances of the book designer's pagination scheme. Either way, it will alter your mind and your life.

Each adventure improved me—enhanced me, even—like a radioactive spider bite. But even conquering mountains on a bicycle that weighs less than a hedonist's guilt—even surviving tattoo removal, a mullet, National Poetry Month, chipmunks, my student loans drying up, and spring training baseball—even writing a column (on deadline, mind you) for several years—did not quite prepare me for writing this Introduction.

No, that took actually sitting down (thanks, bicycle training!) and writing it. I'm happy that I could reward your time and, ideally, the full price you paid with a guiding light by which to understand this book's Unifying Themes and Greater Purposes. If you figure out what that light is, please let me know, so I can include it in future revised editions.

On the right wall had been written:
  I BELIEVE IN EVERYTHING; NOTHING IS SACRED.
And on the left wall:
  I BELIEVE IN NOTHING; EVERYTHING IS SACRED.

— Tom Robbins,
Even Cowgirls Get the Blues

Cracking the
Health Nut

I TAKE PRETTY GOOD CARE of my body. I floss before every dentist appointment, and I stretch so regularly that I even touched my toes once. So you should absolutely take me seriously when I tell you that I have no idea what, exactly, is the normal condition of my prostate.

No one ever told me that I have a prostate, and I completed four whole levels of sex education in school, plus three extended stints in Europe and several rounds of the board game Operation. I used to think—and I am surely not alone here—that prostates were ingrown twins that were carried to term inside old man bodies.

That changed recently, when I met an intrepid fellow in his forties. Let's call him "Tom," because that is his name. Tom survived the youngest case of prostate cancer his doctor had ever seen. So I may not be that far from the abyss, seeing as I am closer to my forties than I have ever been before, while also being farther from them than I will ever be again.

I then became even more aware during prostate cancer's very own entire Awareness Month, when, for thirty topsy-turvy days, prostate cancers the world over gain consciousness, like self-aware robots or Frosty the Snowman. If ever I needed to evaluate my prostate, that time is now, before it comes to life one day..

I asked Tom what I, an exceptional specimen of a young-ish guy, could do to prevent my prostate from swelling like a marshmallow in the microwave. He shared with me the importance of a regular physical checkup for men.

I do not relish scheduling my regular physical checkup for men. It's a lot like getting the oil changed in my car; if I neglect to do it, nothing will go wrong that AAA couldn't fix, if only I had AAA. But why ask someone else to do it at all? This is America, the land of self-reliance. So I opted to explore my own options first. Change my own oil, as it were. I felt around my junk—

Wait. When discussing medical health, a mature vocabulary ensures clarity and accuracy.

So. I conducted a self-examination of my nifkin, prodded my grundle, and discovered that despite three full decades of fiddling with my fiddle, I did not have a clue what equipment I kept in the bottom of my duffel bag. I couldn't pinpoint what might be my prostate, let alone whether or not it was sentient.

Thank goodness for the modern technological wonders tentatively named "the internet" and "Congress," which together dictate everything I need to know about my well-being. With their moral support, I stayed up til the wee hours researching the symptoms of my prostate. It seems to be in good health, unless of course it's not.

As if I didn't have enough to worry about, now I also feel fatigued after all this research, which is a sure sign of one or more other illnesses. I can't even call in sick, because no one would fill in for me and you would not have this book to read.

If you sympathetic readers are anything like the Darling Girlfriend, you're probably saying, "There's a clinical term for people like you who needlessly worry over and self-diagnose an array of highly unlikely diseases, disorders, injuries, and maladies." Yes, I know this term. In fact, it is such a good term that it's actually two terms: Health Nut, wherein "nut" most strictly means "enthusiast."

I am a certified Health Nut because I care greatly about figuring out how to never die, or, more important, how to never ever have a needle stuck in my arm. Yet unpronounceable ailments from the unwiped handles of grocery store shopping carts assail me—and my prostate—at every turn.

Sometimes, an expert opinion truly is best. Since it's difficult to arrange an audience with a congressperson, I now realize I should go to the doctor's office to get the opinion of a trained and well-Vaselined latex glove before I examine myself raw.

But no matter how much I have aggravated this here maybe-it's-a-prostate-but-what-if-it's-actually-a-mislocated-appendix, I cannot persuade the doctor to see me sooner than next month. If I have a medical emergency, the staff helpfully reminds me, I can visit the emergency room. Otherwise, I will have to wait like everybody else for my scheduled appointment or death, in no particular order and subject to approval from my insurance provider.

As frustrating as this healthcare system is, I will follow through with the doctor's appointment, mostly because it will appease the Darling Girlfriend. But I now understand why certain political representatives want to abolish all health care in this great nation for entirely altruistic reasons.

Should they succeed, this Health Nut will help them diagnose their ailments when they arise. But if they need advice on their prostates, Tom recommends a great hands-on grease monkey.

Smartphoney

I HAVE RECENTLY TURNED MYSELF ON to the concept of mindfulness. The basic idea behind mindfulness is to become fully present and engaged with one's own body, thoughts, emotions, and surroundings in any given moment. I am in love with this calm and connected perspective on life. In fact, everywhere I go, I keep reading all about mindfulness on my phone.

I recently got my very first smartphone. I held out through the beta-testing stages of smartphone development, up to and including when Apple ceased to number its iPhones with actual numbers, until it became clear that I would not spend my entire life looking for a place to charge it. Now that I'm on board, let me tell you, this new approach to engaging with the world around me has changed my life. I'm already talking about my phone like other people talk about their cats.

My newest goal is to evangelize the joy of smartphones to both remaining people who have not yet heard of them— plus, the larger demographic of those stubborn Luddites clinging to outdated notions of a telephone longer than I did.

"Telephones were invented for text messaging and for lighting your way to the bathroom in the dark!" is how people justify their flip phones in the face of progress. These people are simply being unmindful of the technological present. They are clinging to the past and not living in the moment, which I now do by taking photographs of information on my computer screen that I want to save for later.

In my old troglodyte days, I was always looking off to the future. "Where will my life be in ten or twenty years?" I wondered. "And also, when can I check baseball scores?"

No longer, muchachos! The smartphone enables me to remain engaged in the present. I am fully aware of where I am—say, a peaceful subalpine forest, with the aspen leaves quivering into estival shades of living joy—while at the very same time cursing an umpire's blindness.

No matter whether I am in that forest, at the grocery store, or trucking down the highway with the cruise control on, this handy little device keeps me connected to the world around me in every conceivable direction. Why, as I write these very words, I am listening to archival broadcasts of Wimbledon matches, rescheduling my regular physical checkup for men, receiving real-time photographs of my mother's dog, and striving vehemently to stay connected to a Wi-Fi signal. And I am giving each distraction my full attention! It's incredible. Technology is like magic, only with autocorrect.

Of course, like any brand-new technology, the smartphone has downsides. Those are, generally, that the phone is unclear in its communication. I will be downloading an app for checking weather while looking into what exactly is a Snapchat anyway, and suddenly my phone will beep like R2-D2 at a surprise birthday party. But it won't tell me why.

Maybe it downloaded updates? Maybe it successfully received a transmission with the stolen plans to the Death Star? Maybe I pressed the beep-boop-beep button? I, as the telephone operator, have no way of knowing.

But the reasons to curse at my phone are far outnumbered by the reasons I will never ever let it out of my sight again. The number one reason I love my smartphone is, as I mentioned, that I can ... something. Was it count my calories? Look up a margarita recipe? Calculate the precise difference in GPS coordinates from my living room to my toilet?

No! Mindfulness. That's it. I can read all about mindfulness everywhere I go.

Mindfulness is a lifelong practice. Mindful people take years and years to awaken to their experiences. It can take this long to learn to view your feelings without judgment or criticism. I think waiting is the worst, though. I hate the frustration of waiting. So thank goodness I've received an express course in mindfulness. After all, there's an app for it.

My ultimate mindfulness is why this particular section reads so clearly, so powerfully, and so free of autocorrected miss takes. It may even win me a Pulitzer for its consciousness-expanding commentary, but who am I to plant that idea in the minds of the prize board? To be honest, I'm not even concerned with awards and acclaim. I'm much more concerned with finding a power outlet, pronto.

The Unsinkable Friendship

SO I HEAR THAT ADULT-AGED PEOPLE have a ton of trouble finding other adult-aged people for romantic and/or sexy times. While I sympathize with the plight of the lovelorn, I think the whole can't-find-a-date-for-Friday-night problem is overblown. Unlikely people fall in love in movies all the time. But I rarely see movies where people fall in friendship.

That's because friends, unlike manholes, aren't just strewn about on the street for people to trip into headfirst. At least the quest for love is filled with tried-and-true techniques, such as buying flowers, passing notes with *yes* and *no* checkboxes, and relying on established patriarchal expectations. Would-be lovers get personal ads and online dating services and local magazines running "Hot Singles" editions, all of which totally always work out.

For those of us seeking friendship, though, we're adrift on a choppy sea, the rudder of companionship sheared off, holes torn in the hull of our confidence, with no end to this metaphor in sight.

Which is why I'm going to spotlight the most eligible friend I know—myself—in the first-ever-that-I-know-of

Q&A Profile for Eligible Friends. Perhaps, by the end of this feature, you will want to be my friend!

> **Q:** Tell us, Zach, why are you interested in finding long-lasting friendship?

> **A:** Because I feel that life is like one of those popsicles with two sticks.

> **Q:** And you want someone to share the other half of the popsicle with you?

> **A:** No, I'll eat the whole thing myself. I just want someone to help break it apart without expecting a foot rub in return, so I can go back to watching the Auto Manufacturer Snack Food Carbonated Beverage Sporting Event in peace.

> **Q:** The prospective friends among our readers are all dying to know: what are your favorite activities?

> **A:** Let me tell you, I am such an impressive potential friend that I have many favorite activities to list. These include reading, talking to my houseplants, and downing an entire bag of tortilla chips in one sitting.

> **Q:** Those don't sound like very friend-conducive activities.

> **A:** I also play guitar.

> **Q:** Excellent! That's an activity you can share with friends. What style of guitar do you play?

> **A:** Air guitar.

> **Q:** Oh.

A: In the shower.

Q: Many people enjoy the great outdoors with friends. What are your favorite outdoor pursuits?

A: I enjoy yelling at chipmunks in my garden. And when they ignore me, I throw stones at them.

Q: That doesn't sound very friendly. Why do you do that?

A: Because there are no children in my neighborhood to throw rocks at instead.

Q: Do you ski? Rock climb? Hike?

A: I ride a bike.

Q: Perfect! There are lots of avid cyclists who would love to be your friend! What do you enjoy most about bicycling?

A: I love that I can feel connected with nature, at one with the breeze through my helmet and the earth under my wheels. But my absolute favorite part is that I can go for hours and hours without having to talk to anybody.

Q: You do realize that the primary part of having friends is being around actual people, right?

A: Oh, sure.

Q: Well, is there anything at all that you enjoy doing with other people?

A: Friendships aren't all about "doing things" with other people. I think you've confused me for one of those "Hot Singles." Asking about someone's day, striving to become a better person—that's all mushy foreplay stuff. And it's way easy, compared to making friends as an adult.

Q: How so?

A: Think about how you can be friends over literally anything as a kid—you both want to play with the same jump rope? Bam! Instant friendship. And that's how we pick up on each other, too. "You like Gruyère? I like Gruyère! Let's go on a date!" But it's not like I, as a seemingly-grown-up individual, can walk up to another guy and say, "You drive on radial tires? I drive on radial tires! Want to hang out?"

We are not doing this Q&A to find true love. We're here to find friends. And unlike romantic interests who will lie about cheese preferences in hopes of ensuing kinky times, true friends will accept us as we are. I am a recluse. And it's incredibly difficult for me, as a hermit, to put myself out there.

Q: Wow. I never stopped to consider the emotional fragility of someone like you trying to make friends.

A: Tell me about it. And I have it double tough, because on top of all that, I just don't like people.

Q: There you have it! If you still think you want to befriend Zach, write a letter to the publisher of this book.

A: Or better yet, don't. This bag of chips ain't big enough for the both of us.

Space Invaders

I NEVER SHOULD HAVE PRESUMED I was friendless. It turns out that I do have friends. And they both decided to spend a night at my house.

It's a miracle these two people—I'll call them "Andy" and "Kristen," because those are their names—even know where I live. I generally don't share more than the two-letter state code of my address, lest the federal student loan thugs find me and repo my formal education. But I seem to have acquired too many manners while on my parents' generous eighteen-year full-ride scholarship prior to pursuing higher ed. Over the holidays, I suggested that Andy and Kristen were always welcome to stay with me, should they ever pass through the municipality of ██████████████.

Lo, not a week hence, I received a request from them—and I quote—to "crash" at my "place."

Let me go on the record saying that I love my friends. I swear this with my hand on the Merriam-Webster dictionary, because it is the thickest and dustiest book in arm's reach at the moment. Heck, I was the best man at their wedding, even though they forbade me to hire strippers, or naked people

13

of any profession whatsoever, for the ceremony. So when I point out that roadside motels were created for the sole purpose of not having out-of-town friends lodge at one's abode, I point it out with purity in my heart.

The same goes for when I mention in passing that some wise tinkerer designed air mattresses to squeak with every toss and squeal with every turn; to sink the sleeper slowly, imperceptibly, onto the cold, hard ground; in short, to sufficiently punish any friends who failed to book a room elsewhere.

The problem is not with having friends sleep in my living room, per se. Nor is it with their parking in my driveway, eating my food, bathing with my soap, clogging my drain with their hair, standing on my bath mat, drying themselves with my towels, tampering with my thermostat, breathing my air, or drinking my special imported beer that I never could find in ███████████ until suddenly it appeared and made my life complete.

No, the problem is that, as someone's grandma advised, you never want to wear worn-out underwear in public, because in the case of an accident you don't want the paramedics to see your holes. Well, my entire home is like a finally-broken-in pair of undies. It exists to make me—and solely me—comfortable. And no one is supposed to see inside.

With guests, I have to move out of my threadbare silk chonies and into Queen Elizabeth's starched ruffles. I know you know precisely what I'm talking about. On a normal day, *you* never fuss over the dust mites breeding behind the bookcase. *You* don't care how much boiled-over (and therefore sterilized) soup is caked on the stovetop. *You* never trip over the jack-o'-lantern in the foyer, and *you* always believed it would stop smelling eventually.

But your guests might notice these things, and they might care! Therefore, you are obligated under the ordinances of the Monroe Doctrine to scrub the ceiling, burnish the door hinges, take out a hit on the neighbor's noisy dog, wash the dishes, and frequent the toilet at the gas station down the road, all to ensure your visitors do not judge you as a human being living like any normal human being who doesn't get out that much.

Sometimes, when a person is hosting friends and doesn't technically start cleaning until the evening of their arrival, that person must make tough choices. I had time for one (1) task and, under the circumstances, I chose the most prudent: I alphabetized my vinyl record collection.

You may scoff at my choice, but I have never lost my entire music collection to a computer crash. And if I have learned one thing about entertaining friends, it's that no one sits around listening to the kitchen sink. Besides, in a pinch, Cat Stevens can lull absolutely anybody to sleep.

As with most anxieties in life, Andy's and Kristen's visit went much more smoothly than anticipated. I greeted them in downtown ███████████ and took them to a restaurant that once passed a health inspection. They got inebriated enough that they would have slept in the car; instead, I drove them to my house and guided them to the air mattress.

Of course, I blindfolded them for the drive. Just because we've been friends for fifteen years doesn't mean I *trust* these people. They could be Department of Education spies for all I know! To be safe, I'll have to relocate, which means I will lose any acquaintances I have left when I ask them to help move these boxes of vinyl.

A Wrinkle in Prime

IN CASE YOU HAVE NEVER BEFORE QUESTIONED my sanity, I am riding in the Iron Horse Bicycle Classic once more this weekend. The purpose of this event is to pedal—using one's own legpower—fifty miles and more than six thousand feet in elevation gain over two toes of the Rocky Mountains. The spirit of the event is to do so without hitching a ride or horking on the other participants.

Been there, done that, right? Not right! This year, I added a new wrinkle to my training regimen, or if you look really closely, lots of new wrinkles: I got old.

I have always looked forward to being old. Old men can wear dapper tweed clothes, and smoke pipes, and flirt with the waitstaff, and fart at Thanksgiving dinner, and generally say anything they want while feigning total hearing loss when anyone complains.

I'm not exactly rushing into my golden years. But by investing in these eventual perks, I am ensuring my future quality of life more reliably than any standard retirement portfolio. Why wait for the Irish Republican Army to blow my funds? I always donate my spare change to myself. Especially during bike season.

I'm not even talking about paying for Spandex shorts and other performance enhancers. I'm talking about springing for bicycle maintenance. A standard-issue road bike requires more attention than a thoroughbred. Practically every time I scrabble onto my bicycle, it makes a new and unsettling sound.

I'm no machine whisperer, so I cannot always determine whether the sound is a handlebar falling off or frogs chirping in a puddle somewhere in the woods off the side of the road. But I am pretty certain that some of these "click" and "pop" and "takatakatakatik" and "ba-DUNK" sounds are genuinely located within the bike itself.

When these noises crop up, I do what the professional blood-transfusing cyclists do: I ignore them and keep riding. Any problem, whether bicyclical or more intimate, is more likely to vamoose on its own than under the influence of my tampering.

Sometimes, though, the noise persists. This is when I try to "isolate the sound." Some questions to ask when isolating the sound include: Does the "queeeeek-queeeeek" happen every time I turn the pedal, or every time the wheel completes a rotation? Is the "crik-pop" happening with every exertion, or only the times I am actually in motion? Am I certain, positively and definitely, the sound is not my own breathing? With these answers, I can Google such precise terminology as "the part of the bike that makes my fingers dirty when I touch it."

Then I visit one of the bicycle shops in town. You know The Guys at bicycle shops; they all fix their own plumbing without checking YouTube first. The Guys always encourage me to describe the issue with sound effects. I'm pretty sure they secretly record my diagnoses and play them at their Mechanically Inclined Dude Rallies.

Before you ask why I don't bring the bike to make its own noises: I can't. The bike has performance anxiety. It only makes sounds when it will embarrass me in front of other cyclists.

"Hmm," The Guys say in manly chorus. "Sounds like your bottom bracket needs replaced. Or if you're lucky, just greased." Now I generally don't have need to grease anything more complex than a frying pan. I also have no idea if a bottom bracket is a real thing that has been invented. The competencies I have spent my life honing, such as finding typos in newspapers, do not require a working knowledge of gadgets more complex than a card catalogue. That's why I hire The Guys in the first place. So they sell me a tool I may or may not be qualified to use, a specialized device that costs more than all three of my other tools combined, and send me on my way.

A gentleman doesn't disassemble and tell. Good thing, then, that this rogue has no working idea what, exactly, he disassembled. Suffice it to say, he got actual grease under his cuticles. And then he tried standing up. There—the culprit! The confounded sound! Coming from bike level!

He crouched back down. The sound again! But then it stopped, until he stood up again. There! A krikking sound! Emanating from ... upon closer inspection ... his own two knees.

Egads. I nearly called it quits, except that the Iron Horse registration fee is non-refundable. Also, for as old as I must be to have crickets in my knee joints, I am but a Cretaceous chicken to the Triassic Thotobolosauruses who pass me on the road.

These wizened cyclists have been old for a *long time*. If they can climb these Colorado mountains, anyone else with creaky legs and a fuzzy memory can, too. So I'm not throwing in my towel. I'm riding over those mountains all the way to the finish line, where I will receive a complimentary T-shirt. I hope it goes dandy with tweed.

Camp Huustupidideawassis Aneewae

As I write this, I am camping all alone, by myself, for the very first time. Flying solo, as it were, like Meriwether Lewis, Buzz Aldrin, the Sundance Kid, Art Garfunkel, and other classic American frontiersmen who ventured forth to become men all by themselves. They didn't have fathers to pitch the tent, or girlfriends to chop the firewood, or famous partners to steal shares of their glory.

My first impression of becoming a man is that tents really have come a long way since my childhood. For instance, tents now have floors. They also promise right there on the packaging not to siphon rain directly into your shoes.

What tents are not now is any easier to assemble. Sure, the camping store offers high-end pop-up tents even quicker to unfurl than a condom on prom night. But this is the wilderness, dagnubbit—it is meant for rugged men experiencing nature through their slowly deflating air mattresses. It is not meant for making camping "easy."

While giving tent setup an initial try, I found a lot of left-behind tent stakes among the pine needles. These stakes could be merely relics from simpler days, when campers torched their floorless tents rather than pack them out. But I know better. These stakes are all that remain of campers eaten by cougars.

Cougars present a very real threat in this campground. The freshly laminated warning signs stapled to the vault toilet by the Department of Game & Fish describe how cougars want to bat me around like a mouse in a pinball machine.

If the government would only supply the cougars with giant cardboard boxes to play in, they'd stay occupied for basically ever. But federal funding is tight, even considering the influential work of the camping lobby. So I must stake my survival on these actual posted tips:

- Avoid jogging, hiking, or walking alone.
- Avoid jogging or hiking at dusk or at dawn.
- In fact, why don't you just avoid moving at all, ever.
- If you do move, carry a sturdy walking stick.
- NEVER APPROACH A COUGAR!

Despite my best efforts to avoid cougars, it's really quite difficult when camping alone to eat s'mores without moving. So in the event I attract a cougar anyway, the signs suggest to treat it the same way I would a grade-school bully, ideally before it crushes me into Fancy Feast. These tips are especially encouraging, because some of them are in all caps and others use title case:

- STOP! STAY CALM!
- Do Not Run! Face the cougar & stand tall.
- If cougar approaches, throw objects & speak loudly.

And, most helpfully of all:

- If cougar attacks—Fight Back!

Now, according to my imagination, a mountain lion is larger than the average housecat whose claws I cannot remove from my clothing without it shredding me like an expired check. Of course I won't Fight Back. Are you kidding? If a cougar attacks me, I plan to flop into a boring heap and hope that, before I regain consciousness, the cougar moves on to other feline activities, such as attacking itself or sleeping.

You might think that only cowards faint instead of Fighting Back. But that's not true. Cowards would read these warning signs and promptly return to town under the guise of fetching all the camping essentials they just realized they forgot. I am no coward. I will test my mettle without such frivolities as can openers or a pillow or breakfast. I will make do with what I brought, or do without.

And I think I'll be doing without, unless my phone magically discovers a signal out here so I can call the tent manufacturer or maybe my parents to walk me through putting this tent together before darkness blankets the forest which is already happening and there's noises in the trees and no sign of the local ranger and it's so dark I can't even see what I'm writing anymore if you all discover this notebook after I die please tell everyone I loved them and I'm sorry about that unfortunate incident with the beans ....

I'm back and clearly not dead yet. In the end, I bucked up to the challenge. I worked up quite a macho sweat threading the tent poles through the tent pole sleeves. I correctly oriented the rainfly in less than five tries. Not to brag, but I even triple-pinned the tent zippers shut with all the extra stakes lying around. I'm admiring the whole installation as I write by lanternlight inside it.

I have a big stick; I'm not moving; and I challenge any hungry cougar to tear through this manly fortress and take its chances with me. No, really, please; I'm not sure how I'll get out of here otherwise.

Voting Tool

WITH LESS THAN FOUR YEARS TO GO until the next presidential election, we are finally more than halfway through the current campaign season. Hallelujah! However, the ticking clock means that, as a Responsible Citizenry, we must begin to pay attention to the serious issues as reported to us by seriously way too many campaign emails.

But even the most effective spam filter can't keep up with all the opinions we're supposed to take seriously. So to make your voting decisions straightforward, accessible, and mindless, I hereby offer Hot Takes on how you should feel about the most pressing and timeless campaign issues.

STUDENT LOANS

"Biff" says he wants a college education. But "Biff" hears that student loan debt in this country has reached $1.2 trillion. This number is due in part to the rising cost of a successfully corporatized college education, and in another part to the federal government loaning students their tuition money at rates comparable to those of any respectable shark.

Some candidates want to lower these interest rates. Some want college to be free, as if college is a natural extension of a free high school education.

HOT TAKE: If my Greek serves, this great land is founded on *E pluribus unum*—"you need money to make money." So if "Biff" cannot even afford college on his own at the adult age of almost eighteen, then he should not expect a profitable career after college.

Plus, we live in a democracy that politely requests our participation with the simple act of voting. Yet all throughout childhood, "Biff" did not vote a single time in any federal election. You think "Biff" deserves a handout now?

Speaking of money for nothing ...

EQUAL PAY FOR WOMEN

"Lakshmi" recently discovered that she makes less money per hour than her male counterparts, although she works more effectively. "Lakshmi" thinks she deserves pay commensurate with her skill set, and some apparently serious presidential contenders agree with her.

HOT TAKE: Of course "Lakshmi" earns less money than men doing the same work. Women are, on average, shorter than men. Furthermore, women have a greater life expectancy. They therefore have more earning potential.

The wage discrepancy is more than offset with the money women can make—without any male competition!—during those peak employment years between the ages of seventy-six and eighty-one. We poor, fragile men have to earn what money we can while we are still alive.

You think that's not reason enough? Fewer men populate the United States than women. Taken collectively, men make the same amount as all women combined, if you discount the overage.

It's just like how the wealth of the masses is balanced out by a very few rich folks. The rich *have* to hoard a lot of money to offset the billions, if not thousands, of dollars that all the poorer people spread among themselves.

It's time ladies like "Lakshmi" realize they are part of the majority power in this country. They need to stop seizing control from those minority individuals who enjoy less life and, therefore, less liberty and less happiness.

So get with it, "Lakshmi."

Speaking of equal distributions ...

CORPORATE HUMAN RIGHTS

"Flor-Mart" is a moderately successful multi-billion-dollar company. It stimulates the economy in all the places it most likes being stimulated. It employs countless "Biffs" and "Lakshmis" who cannot afford college, and it pays them commensurate with their life expectancies. "Flor-Mart" is an upstanding citizen, according to the Supreme Court and everything.

But certain campaign staffers compose nasty emails that propose taking away "Flor-Mart's" right to engage in the democratic process. They want to limit "Flor-Mart's" ability to speak its mind. They even want to belittle "Flor-Mart's" personhood, as if "Flor-Mart" is an undocumented immigrant or an unconceived fetus.

HOT TAKE: You probably have stuff you want to do with your life, right? Raise children, go camping, watch Netflix, buy beer for your favorite writer. But those things take time, and you do not have time. Enter Flor-Mart! Corporate individuals like Flor-Mart make all the meaningless decisions for you so you don't have to. They streamline your options for what food to eat, which celebrities to gossip about, what clothes are available to wear, which events the news media covers, and which creation myths to study in school.

These favors enable a Responsible Citizenry to live free lives. This streamlined divestment is the greatest public service since *Sesame Street*—which, by the way, has always been funded by the Corporation for Public Broadcasting, itself a corporation if names are to be believed. Better a corporation than the government! You cannot trust the government's motives when it funds public services. Know who you *can* trust, who doesn't have any interest in profiting off basic public services? Corporations!

Stay strong, "Flor-Mart." With your example, we are set to vote in some future election or other. Please email me when it's over.

Bushwhacked

REMEMBER THAT DISTANT TIME on social media, when people everywhere dumped ice water on their heads to raise public awareness of people dumping ice water on their heads? Those folks bullied into the so-called Ice Bucket Challenge were required, according to entirely arbitrary rules, either to drench themselves in an arctic shower or to donate money to the ALS Association.

I, alone among humankind, refused the challenge when put to it. I did so because I do not personally know what the initials ALS stand for.

In the name of Responsible Reporting, I conducted exhaustive research on the front page of the ALS Association's website. It helpfully informed me that the Association is continually dedicated to raising money through the Ice Bucket Challenge, without actually spelling out what ALS means.

I would sure hate to give undue backing to something like the Antique Lederhosen Society, especially when there are other worthy causes, such as funding research into specific cancers that affect people dear to me.

I felt good and principled by refusing to participate. Then, out of the blue, Pops, my dear DNA donor, Ice Bucket Challenged me. I needed an ironclad shield to deflect this personal blow, lest I come across as anti-ALS research or, worse, a scaredy-pants chicken butt. So as a rugged individualist, an honorable and incorruptible scoundrel, I decided that I do not, under any circumstances no matter how noble, give in to peer pressure.

I tested my resolve on a short family vacation. Figuring that Pops would give me grief for "wussing out" like a "punk," I prepared my anti-peer pressure spiel. But he said not a word about the Ice Bucket Challenge.

What a relief! His silence gave me paternal affirmation, exactly what every nonconformist wants for Christmas besides a leather jacket. He must have been delighted that I did not cave to his pressure.

Pops suggested we take an afternoon stroll together. I took this dudely jaunt up the road, quality father-son time, as a clear show of his pride.

We stumbled upon a trailhead pointing up one of the local neighborhood mountains. "Let's take a little hike," Pops said. "Why not?"

I voiced several reasons why not, including a lack of water bottles, improper footwear, looming storm clouds, nobody knowing where we were, and bears.

"So what, man?" Pops said. "It'll be fun."

He had a point. I didn't know what the point was, but I wasn't about to admit that. Besides, any real individualist such as my new and improved self didn't worry about trivial concerns like hydration and wildlife.

We conquered that mighty ascent, sure enough. I even went slow, so as to let Pops think he was leading the way. It was the least I could do to thank him for appreciating my rebel blood.

Atop the summit, we admired the rocky, scraggly landscape below us until I got vertigo. "You want to bushwhack down?" Pops asked.

What should a rugged maverick like me say to that? The forest ranger who spoke to my class in elementary school made it clear that if we ever stepped a foot off the trail, we would commit some foul deed like crushing the wings of a butterfly, causing unimaginable repercussions into the distant future. Also, we would be fed to Smokey.

Before I answered, Pops said, "Nothing ventured," and he skipped over the edge like a particularly balding bighorn sheep without finishing the thought. Nothing ventured ... what? Nothing sprained, stranded, lost, or devoured by feral dogs?

I wondered if I should fetch a helicopter airlift team. But if Pops died alone before we saved him, it would raise serious questions about my motives when I executed his will. So I pursued him down the slope to rescue him myself.

This—sliding down rock faces, picking a path through strands of scrub oak thick enough to hide a whole host of bears—this was how free-wheeling folks ought to live. Scuffling down a mountain liberated me from all the online fads that coerce susceptible minds into doing brainless and even dangerous deeds. My renegade spirit roared every time I hugged a lightning-struck tree to plan my next step.

Bound by the Masculine Code of Manly Explorers, I am not at liberty to discuss how I led us back to civilization. It might have involved heroics against bobcats and a daring descent down a cliff without the aid of a single YouTube how-to video. Yet made it we did, bloodied and dusty and really, really hot.

In lieu of my preferred flavored sports drink, Pops mixed up a congratulatory bucket of ice water for me to dump over myself. He even recorded the cooling-off celebration to share with all his friends. I intend to use this videographic proof of my triumph to spread awareness of A Very Worthy New Movement, which will make the world impervious to bullying tactics. The method is simple: be like me and don't give in to peer pressure. I dare you.

Squashed
Dreams

THE DAYLIGHT HOURS ARE GETTING SHORTER, the holiday season is bearing down upon us, and all consumer goods from hot dogs to Honda Accords will soon come with pumpkin spice flavoring. But not everything this time of year need be tainted by such doom and gloom.

For instance, autumn is also the season when plants die. In their stead, they leave behind delicious plant babies for us humans to eat. Home gardeners today share in a long-running tradition with humankind's original farmers. The experience is precisely the same, except that, to our pioneering forebears on the Oregon Trail computer game, failure meant dysentery and to us, it means eating peanut butter with a spoon. At least *they* got to hunt an excess of bison.

Yet despite forgoing all the fun parts of the frontier lifestyle, I sacrificed an entire late summer evening to bring you Foolproof Tips for raising and butchering your own little vegetable orphans.

First and foremost, you must know that unattended squash plants will engulf an entire yard and possibly the neighbor's cat. This is true even if you don't actually plant squash. You might reasonably assume these unexpected sprouts are marijuana, and thus you let them grow unchecked until it is far too late for Mr. Farklebottoms. But you unwittingly do your crops a favor and discover

Foolproof Tip #1: Never declare defeat, even when your garden breaks rank.

At first unwanted, a ground cover of Surprise Squash! allows you to let nature run its course, until such time as you rent a Caterpillar machine to uproot it all.

The brazen amateur farmer might declare Mission Accomplished at this point. However, you still have enemies to contend with, and they will teach you

Foolproof Tip #2: At the first sign of chipmunks, declare defeat.

Quicker than you can throw rocks at them, these pitiless pillagers will devour every one of your crops down to stumps—except, of course, the squash.

It is true that, as a modern farmer, your anti-rodent arsenal is formidable. You have opposing thumbs, chemical technology, bird netting, and a three-inch vertical leap. But chipmunks have speed. They have sharp teeth. And they don't scream and jump on chairs when you sneak up on them. This leads you to

Foolproof Tip #3: Just let go. You're not in control of nature. So instead, appreciate its ruthless beauty and accept gardening for what it really is: a valid reason to drink beer outside.

Besides, you could always have it worse. Instead of a chipmunk problem, you could have a grizzly bear problem.

Today, 1,850 musky, rippled grizzly bears tear up the continental United States. Another fifty-five thousand or so roam Canada and Alaska.

Some of us—let's call ourselves "people who value our limbs"—are quite content with the grizzly bear status quo. But an actual group, which I read about in a newspaper so it must be real, is petitioning the U.S. Fish and Wildlife Service to *expand* the grizzly bear recovery plan. These people want to move grizzlies to New Mexico, Colorado, California, Utah, and—in a menacing blow to anti-immigrant forces—Arizona.

Why bother? I'm thinking, grizzly bears must be happy right where they are. They are tough critters, nearly as ferocious as the hungry chipmunks who have no problem colonizing your garden. If the grizzlies really wanted the Grand Canyon, they could just take it. I for one wouldn't stand in their way.

Other people are, to put it tactfully, crazier than I am. "Grizzly bears were here *fiiiiiiirst*," whine groups like the above-mentioned, as if that defense is valid in a court of law higher than the first grade. Saber-toothed tigers and wooly mammoths were here even earlier, but you don't see nearly as many people clamoring for their reintroduction. And the chipmunks beat me here, but that doesn't give them the right to ruin my rutabagas!

I must be honest, though. The more I skim articles about grizzly bears, the more I think of them just like teenagers, only sweeter smelling. They want to eat. They want to roam. And they will fight me if I ask them to turn down their music.

At the end of the day, both teenagers and grizzly bears are living creatures with a striking resemblance to human beings, at least once you peel off their outer layers. The thought softens my heart enough to imagine that, someday, all of earth's uncouth creatures (except the chipmunks) will learn to live in harmony with humans.

If that dream is too lofty for you, then stick to reality by following my Foolproof Tips. They will ensure bounty all winter long. I for one will be dining on plenty of Surprise Squash! with peanut butter.

Let Them Eat Gourds!

IF SOMETHING FAMILY-FRIENDLY CAN BE DONE with a pumpkin, it has been done at the Circleville Pumpkin Show. Circleville is a small town in central Ohio whose most notable feature is that it houses Hivelys, such as my aunt and uncle, thereby disproving that the Midwest is entirely bland. It also puts on the annual Pumpkin Show, a harvest festival that focuses on, you guessed it, corn.

Just joshing! Corn is another Midwestern stereotype. The Circleville Pumpkin Show has focused on pumpkins, and only pumpkins, ever since the mayor started the festival in 1903.

The way I read it, all the area farmers back inna day were wagoning their harvest bounty to town, and the mayor wanted to appreciate their wives' produce. So he set up displays and established a competition for the largest pumpkin grown by a lady. Ever a visionary, the mayor also held a competition for the largest pumpkin grown by regular guy farmers, thereby striving for gender equality a full century before we still don't have it today.

Big pumpkins are the main attractions at the Show. The primary difference today is that the pumpkins are approximately the size of oxen, and they eat more, too. Otherwise, Pumpkin Show is precisely how I remember it from when I first visited it at age thirteen, except that now I know the meaning of the word "indigestion."

Which is really too bad, because the festival carries on precisely how the mayor envisioned it more than a hundred years ago, with the world's largest pumpkin pie, pumpkin waffles, pumpkin pizza, pumpkin ice cream, pumpkin chili, pumpkin donuts, pumpkin pulled-pork sandwiches, pumpkin cappuccinos, pumpkin kettle corn, the face-painted Pumpkin Show Man navigating crowds on rollerblades, carnival games where you can win a Justin Bieber poster, and beauty pageant competitions for the Pumpkin Show queen.

This fall, my uncle wanted me to have the full Pumpkin Show experience as an adult with access to antacids. He signed me up to sell pumpkin coffee and ride on a parade float alongside eight strangers and a roasted chicken. He took my picture under the "Most Unusual Pet" parade placard. But, despite wanting me to have the full Pumpkin Show experience, he did not enter me for the Miss Pumpkin Show competition.

So, in the spirit of still striving for gender equality, here is my at-large application for next year's crown, answering the same questions asked of my competition.

Miss Pumpkin Show Application

Entrant:

Miss Zach Hively

Age:

30ish (a lady never tells!)

Hobbies:

Doing family-friendly things to pumpkins,
such as sawing them open with serrated knives,

gutting them, and displaying their corpses to the neighborhood. I also enjoy consuming their flesh from tin cans.

Plans after high school:

Ride the bus home, eat a sandwich, probably take a nap.

Favorite Pumpkin Show memory:

There are so many wonderful memories to choose from! Like that time I would have won the pumpkin toss if I had forged my age to enter the kids' twelve-and-under category. Or that time I sat on the announcement stage for a parade, and the man with the microphone kept insisting that my aunt "do the mayor when he comes by."

But I have to go with the 1998 pet parade. My uncle loaned us the gerbil tank from the school where he works. Lo, the gerbil had that very morning given birth to half a dozen babies! My sisters, my cousin, and I dragged those gerbils in a wagon through downtown Circleville, and when we returned to the staging area, there was only the mama gerbil left. And boy, was she stuffed.

Somehow, we did not win the Most Unusual Pet category. As Pumpkin Show queen, I will institute a Greatest Attrition category for all future pet parades.

Favorite thing to do at the Pumpkin Show:

Once again, there are just so many choices. But I would have to say my favorite activity is eavesdropping.

Eavesdropping? What do you hear?

I can't tell you! That would be rude. Besides, this year's Baby Parade entrants really aren't as ugly as people said.

What qualities do you have that you believe would make you successful as Miss Pumpkin Show, if chosen for the honor?

Diversity. I would be the first queen to break countless, possibly up to a dozen, glass hurdles. I'd be the first queen with an unplucked beard, and the first on this side of twenty. A real Jackie Robinson in the realm of Pumpkin Show queens.

If you could travel to any event in the United States to promote the Circleville Pumpkin Show, where would it be and why?

The Great American Beer Festival in Denver, Colorado. Seven hundred brewers. Thirty-five hundred beers. Limitless samples.

How would you describe Pumpkin Show to someone who has never experienced it before?

Well, I described it already, so instead, I'd like to offer a new slogan suggestion.

The Circleville Pumpkin Show: Come for the pumpkins, stay for them too! And ladies, please keep your distance from the mayor.

Halloween Hisssterics

HALLOWEEN CENTERS AROUND THE ANCIENT, solemn Celtic rite of taking candy from strangers. I spent Halloween in Ireland once and celebrated by getting too drunk to verify how the Irish observe the holiday in the modern era. But in America, I know for a proven fact that until recently the tradition had not changed in hundreds, perhaps even dozens, of years.

My parents' generation brought Halloween to our shores in what historians refer to as "pilgrim times." Strangers had yet to perfect abduction as an art form, which meant kids could go trick-or-treating after dark, with all the eggs their homemade costumes could carry. Meanwhile, their parents stayed home with the porch lights off, inventing the concept of "sexy Halloween costumes."

In other words, Halloween was so safe it could actually be dangerous. But then some kids walked in on their pirate-clad parents swashing each other's buckles, which traumatized them (the kids) (but also the parents) into cracking down on the holiday. My parents, for instance, not only made me say "thank you" to the strangers who gave me candy, but they made me wait to actually eat any of the candy until approximately February. This gave them the time to visually inspect every piece of candy for concealed razor blades, or poison, or invisibly poisoned razor blades. My mother confiscated so many compromised Heath bars that I'm still afraid to eat one.

Now that Halloween is ruined, we celebrate with the increased paranoia that our youngest, most impressionable citizens will experience actual fun. Reflective tape diminishes the fearsomeness of paper plate masks. Families gather in shopping malls or parking lots before sundown. And I get strange looks and questions about my age that I sure didn't get when I went trick-or-treating back in the day.

Yet while parents today still check candy for poison, they don't check *anywhere* for silent rattlesnakes.

You better beware, gentle readers. Rattlesnakes are evolving under our feet into silent hunters. This is no mere hyperbole, the likes of which *Call Me Zach Hively Because That Is My Name* strives to avoid. Like the Who without Keith Moon, like Led Zeppelin without John Bonham, like me banging on the steering wheel, rattlesnakes are performing sans reliable percussion. Herpetologists in South Dakota are observing an increase in rattlers with atrophied tail muscles, which sure takes the shimmy out of their shake.

This shift is supposedly not the fault of drugs or excessive lifestyles, but of humans. As if we are capable of creating such monsters! These scientists expect us to believe that human beings with shovels and cars and traps and .22 caliber pistols have killed so many fully functional rattlesnakes as to increase the breeding success of their gimpy counterparts.

But the so-called "experts" are sticking to their snakes. So I did some follow-up speculation of my own. I discovered that even if you don't count yourself among South Dakota's seventeen residents, this national crisis could still bite you.

We all ought to know that car dealerships here in the Wild West are crawling with venomous, cold-blooded hunters, as well as snakes. But even places like Ohio have their infestations. Or at least they used to; rattlesnakes there are increasingly really hard to find. Is this scarcity due to their endangered status? Or are the snakes hiding in survivalist-style enclaves among the cornstalks and pumpkins, waiting to inundate unsuspecting lawns on Halloween night? You be the judge, because I have no idea.

It gets even scarier, because there is now such a thing as outer space robot snakes. NASA has taken a long look at sidewinder rattlesnakes to design new devices that can move where lesser machines have to call AAA Emergency Roadside Assistance. One research director notes, with a complete lack of ever having seen a horror movie, that "we have this self-informing system that has really opened up new parameters within snake biology and robotics."

This is hard science, people, and therefore absolutely bound to turn against us. If there's one thing more chilling than alien android rattlesnakes, it's real-world rattlesnakes which are even more aggressive because they can't fend off intruders with their rattles. And if there's one thing more frightening than silent rattlesnakes, it's someone stuffing a silent rattlesnake into your child's candy sack. Fortunately, you can use my mom's ploy and just leave it there until February, or until you've plucked out all the Heath bars. Whichever comes first.

Best in Show

I WAS RIDING MY BICYCLE on a county road outside of town where, unimpeded by houses and buildings, I could see campaign signs for miles. That's when I figured out how to fix our broken election system.

I sometimes ride one of those sleek road bikes made for athletes and other recreational crazy persons. My bike is a lower-end model that nevertheless weighs less than my water bottle thanks to technology discarded by NASA for making their spacecraft too light. Yet despite being designed for atmospheric re-entry, the bike fails to withstand the usual cracks and bumps in the road caused by extreme contractor ineptitude. Also, I have to wear inflexible shoes with protruding plastic pieces that padlock me directly to the pedals.

On this particular ride, the shoehorn that doubles as a seat wobbled loose. I pulled onto the shoulder to assess its mechanics with manly stares. When it failed to tighten itself, I deliberated whether I should secure the seat with chewing gum, or drag the whole contraption to a shop in town where they knew which one of Allen's funny-looking screwdrivers to use.

Before I decided, a small car swerved off the road ahead of me and into the only shoulder space free of campaign signs for six miles in either direction. Evidently, the mud there was too deep even for politicians to mark their territory.

The driver climbed right out of the stuck car—*into* the muck!—and she said, "Rats. I just wanted to let my dog out to pee!"

I wanted to point out that, mere yards away on any side, her dog had a much wider array of targets; he could have highlighted some candidate's TRUST, or splashed the dash in RE-ELECT. Instead, I offered her my cell to phone a tow truck.

She already had one—a phone, not a tow truck—but she did not seem the least interested in calling for help. "We can push it out," she declared.

This was a brilliant idea, and I told her so. But I would be the opposite of help, falling down in the mud with no footing whatsoever, what with my cleated feet and all.

"So why don't I get in the car," I offered gallantly, "and you push!"

I laid my bike on the ground—which probably decalibrated a derailleur or bent a coaxial flange tooth or somehow otherwise further crippled my steed—and pranced over the mud to wedge myself into a front seat more cramped than most iron maidens.

Turned out, the squeeze was so tight because I was sitting halfway atop a disgruntled, full-bladdered dachshund.

Now, some dogs will growl at or attack anyone who isn't Their Human. But this pup understood that I was here to rescue his fair mistress. He scuttled to the passenger seat and observed my operation of the clutch and those other two whatchamacalits, masterful even with clunky bicycle feet. Though the damsel put forth a doughty effort worthy of ten Clydesdales, her car would have remained marooned without my subtle yet crafty steering. Within fifteen minutes, I had rescued her—and her little dog, too.

She tried to thank me, but a hero needs no gratitude. I sped into the sunset, lest the car get stuck again before my bike seat fell off completely. Even Batman knows better than to hang around.

But enough about my chivalry. The point is, we could improve our national and local politics alike if we stopped taking baseless potshots at politicians. We should rather judge them entirely by their dogs.

I have petsitted for enough people to know that animals take on the neuroses of their humans. This is not always a bad thing. Look at the dachshund in the car. He was alert, comfortable, and trusting of a noble stranger. This tells me that I can trust his human. I would accept candy from this woman, without knowing so much as her name, based on the sole fact that the dog showed zero interest in poisoning me.

Sure, with politicians, there is always a risk. Dogs, much like spouses, can be sent to obedience school and chosen purely for their photogenics. However, dogs tend to act much more like vice-presidential candidates than spouses. They will do *anything* on camera, especially if it's precisely what they shouldn't do.

This is how we can glimpse the true character of candidates, unmasked by plastic surgeons and other hardened campaign strategists. We as a nation may not know the first thing about Syrian rebels, but *by god* do we know how to criticize other people's dogs.

In addition, we could boil complex political ideologies down to simple debate-style questions: "Whooza good girl? Huh? Huh? That's right! And whooza good boy?"

I speak for dogkind, and all write-in spaces on your ballot, when I answer: "I am."

Holiday Budgets on the Fly

NOVEMBER ARRIVED EARLIER THAN EVER this year, probably due to global warming. That means it's time for you to kick back and relax for the rest of the season, because your Christmas shopping is already done.

Unless you're like me. I just found out that people my age are technically adults. This classification burdens me with the responsibility of orchestrating a Flawless Holiday Season. Someone should have told me sooner! For I have not started thinking about what presents to give my loved ones, let alone how to make scarecrow table settings out of oak leaves, Q-tips, and leftover jack-o'-lantern scraps.

I'm also discovering the financial strains of the holidays. I haven't yet paid down my Valentine's Day, St. Patrick's Day, Easter, Arbor Day, Administrative Professionals' Week, Memorial Day, Fourth of July, Labor Day, and Indigenous Peoples Day credit card bills. Yet somehow I'm supposed to budget funds for making enough fudge to give to everyone I know. These folks will eventually throw it away because *everyone* is giving them fudge, and they can't pawn it off on the dog without killing it.

Someone has to figure out a way to survive the holidays without going broke. Until someone does, I'll offer you my own Totally Not Miserly Money Tips for a Flawless Holiday Season. If you start now, you can sprinkle your financial creativity piecemeal across the entire season.

Miserless Money Tip #1: Do not get suckered into "selling" your Halloween candy.

Dentists across the nation run a pyramid scheme every year wherein they offer to "buy back" treats. You might think this is a get-rich-quick scheme, wherein you can get rich quickly. You would be wrong. Many dentists, undoubtedly poorer than real doctors, try to buy your candy for coupons, toothbrushes, hygiene kits, and other lame stuff instead of money.

They then ship the candy to troops overseas. This sounds noble, except that no one—not even one's little sister—is dumb enough to trade away the good candy. So dentists send the military entire cases of fruit-flavored Tootsie Rolls, which demoralizes the soldiers, which means the terrorists win and we'll never have Christmas again.

So, please, hang on to your candy. Trust me. You will need the sugar buzz to pull off the next Totally Not Miserly Money Tip with gusto:

Miserless Money Tip #2: Turn to organic landscaping.

Time is money, and responsible homeowners spend entire days raking their lawns and bagging leaves. Or so I hear.

What if, instead of throwing away precious resources, you committed to bettering yourself and the environment? Unlike more time-consuming commitments, this one is simple: Don't rake your lawn. The leaves will degrade naturally and return their nutrients to the soil, thereby improving the long-term health of your property and leaving you more time to watch football.

Yes, your neighbors will complain at first. Seize this moment to offer them your business card (which can be handwritten on the back of a grocery receipt) and explain that you are an Organic Landscaping Consultant. For the entry-level price of several hundred dollars, they too can reap the benefits of healthy living!

At best, you make millions of dollars. At worst, you don't throw out your back raking leaves, and you don't tear holes in your jeans, which is really good because shopping for new jeans is the worst experience I have had all year.

Sturdy, dependable blue jeans used to be the national symbol of America. They reflected our commitment to quality, our dedication to ruggedness, and our national fear of nudity. A man could wear the same pair of jeans his entire life, so long as his wife didn't throw them in a back-alley dumpster while he slept. I myself have owned the same three pairs of jeans since approximately the seventh grade, when I outgrew my sweatpants.

In that time, the recession (and probably climate change too) decimated the jeans industry. All pants now come in hipster styles, which, ironically, don't allow for hips. They also assume that every man has legs like a prepubescent Cindy Crawford. Which I don't. But I *do* have a thirty-one-inch waist, which is *the worst*, because apparently we ship all odd-numbered waistlines overseas along with our reject Halloween candy.

When I finally found a pair of jeans that approximately fit me, the denim promptly ripped, because all jeans now come with the same durability as wet crepe paper.

Anyway, the point is, if you follow these two whole Totally Not Miserly Tips for a Flawless Holiday Season, as well as the ones I forgot because I got angry thinking about blue jeans, then you are guaranteed to survive the holidays without financial stress. This is because you won't have any friends left, and you won't have to buy them presents. Consequently, you won't get any fudge, and your old pants will still fit next year. And that's what really matters.

Medicine
for Dummies

SOME TIME AGO, I wrote about the state of my prostate. The results are in. It turns out that I, despite all of my years eating Flintstones vitamins, am not a qualified health-care professional.

One concerned reader noted that a wellness checkup for men, an important component of keeping doctors in business, is not prostate cancer *prevention* but rather prostate cancer *detection*. I stand corrected, albeit a bit bowlegged after running myself through so many fruitless background checks. And my friend Andy, who is training to be a real doctor, wrote me: "As a medical semi-professional, I can say with confidence that you're too young to need your prostate checked for anything other than recreational purposes."

Despite such assurances, I did not cancel my scheduled wellness checkup, because it was tougher to get than a Tickle-Me Elmo. (Which, now that I think about it, is pretty much what I was looking for.) And if I, a white male with extreme medical concerns, could barely get a doctor's appointment before the end of ~~the next Clinton~~ the Oprah presidency,

I knew that untold other American citizens must be dying out there.

Which they are—nearly seven thousand every day. That's one whole person for every 219 Big Macs sold. When I was born, I did not sign up for a world where people die. Namely, I did not sign up for a world where *I* could die.

If healthcare wasn't going to make me invincible, then by gum, I would. I had already taken matters into my own hands—what I now refer to as "private *detection*." That didn't work. So it was time to take matters into my own mouth.

That's right: I learned CPR. But before you rush out to take CPR classes of your own, you should know that CPR is worthless. Even if you are fully certified, you cannot save your own life. Even so, I stayed for the entire class, because they provided snacks.

And I'm glad I did, because now, should the top half of a mannequin ever collapse to the floor and prove unresponsive —you would be surprised how often this happens, even in a first-world nation—I am trained to provide it with chest compressions and emergency breathing until an instructor calls time.

Ultimately, the class gave me something much more meaningful than a CPR certification card. It endowed me with the skills and the confidence to go into any dangerous, high-stress situation and imagine an even more dangerous and stressful one.

I honed these abilities during the simulations in class. We students concocted difficult scenarios with plenty of hazards, in order to heighten the challenge of giving CPR to a dummy. My finest creation involved a bicycle, bucking horses, an overturned eighteen-wheeler, four dozen youth basketball campers, and a prominent international figure. Doctor-patient confidentiality, not to mention word count, prevents me from describing whether emergency breathing saved the astronaut after her crash landing.

Destroying lives in order to attempt saving them was the most enriching four hours I spent that afternoon. I awaited my own doctor's appointment with an invigorated appreciation for medical practitioners. My doctor and I were basically colleagues now. Peers! Equals in every way, except I am not open to malpractice suits.

I simply had to see my comrade-in-medicine right away, before anyone revoked my CPR certification. I petitioned the nurses until they canceled someone's appointment to slot me in. But lest you get as enthused as I was, I must tell you that a doctor's practice is a really dull way to save lives. Their processes may work fine in theory, but in reality they are much less exciting than your average warrantied toaster oven.

I'm not questioning whether these professionals know what they're doing. All I'm saying is that when the nurse took my pulse, she did not even attempt to invent a life-threatening hazardous situation. Doing so would be *super easy*. Heck, I invented dozens of maladies in the waiting room while filling out the eighty-page medical history questionnaire.

Then the real doctor finally came in. She was a no-nonsense professional who wasted zero time asking me every question I had just answered on the questionnaire. She deemed my responses honest without even running a psych eval or checking if my fingers were crossed behind my back, then declared me healthy and sent me out the door.

Oh, sure, she looked up my nose and put her cold stethoscope on my back. *Boooooorrrring*. I look up my own nose every day! So the lesson is, if you want some real medical drama in your life, yell for CPR in a circus tent frequented by schoolchildren and dignitaries, and then collapse. And if you want the serious recreational hijinks, make an appointment with Andy. He's almost as certified as I am.

Busy to
the Core

FOR TWO THOUSAND SOME-ODD YEARS—the entire period known either as AD, "After Democracy," or CE, the "Congressional Era"—our government has been gridlocked. And Americans are sick and tired of it. We showed in the midterm elections that we finally want to get things done, so long as one of those things isn't voting.

Hey, we never claimed that we wanted to *do* things! We just want them *done*. Take, for example, *Star Wars*. I waited since before the prequels for another real *Star Wars* movie to get done. When Disney bought Lucasfilm, including its intellectual property in the form of George Lucas's brain in a Tupperware, I thought we'd have a new movie by Christmastime. I mean, these are the same Disney folks who wrote *Frozen* in a single weekend.

Instead, it took multiple years to write just the first new movie's title. In case you're not a super-nerd or a human being with the internet, the title of that film is *Star Wars: The Force Awakens*. I suppose it's catchier than *The Force Wakes Up* and truer to the original films than *Star Wars: The Force: The Musical*. But come on. I could write an entire title with more mass appeal, more explosions, and way more implied sexual tension in far less than two years.

Or Disney could have catered to its base with *Star Wars: Hey, Look, We Brought Back Han Solo While Harrison Ford Is Still Medically Alive*. But I'm not in charge of a multi-billion-dollar industrial entertainment conglomerate enterprise, so what do I know?

This is what I know: if you want something done right, you have to put it on a to-do list so you can cross it out.

I write a to-do list every day I remember to do it. In order to feel accomplished by bedtime, I fill the list with routine activities. For instance, on a randomly selected to-do list that I just pulled out of the pocket of my pajama pants, I have yet to cross out "bathe." But I have five lines through "eat a cookie."

As you might suspect, I face a deep self-evaluation when I wake up—or, "awaken"—and look in the mirror each afternoon. I must ask my innermost self: Once I've crossed out all the cookies, how do I manage the rest of my list?

The answer is "prioritizing." Crossing things off a to-do list is not enough to stay productive. I have to prioritize that list so that I clear out space in my fridge before my apples go bad.

You see, my mother gave me about fourteen grocery bags of apples from some stranger's tree. I promptly stuffed them in the fridge and ignored them. But I knew, deep in the back of my brain, that starving children in China would love the fridge they built to be put to better use. So I wrote "Make Applesauce" atop my to-do list.

I love applesauce, particularly because it has zero resemblance to apples. I have never bitten into a spoonful of applesauce and said, "Gee, where should I throw away this apple core when I'm finished?" or, "Shoot, this applesauce turned mealy." Besides, I for one am confident that the process of turning apples into applesauce also turns worms into applesauce.

Yes, it would have been both quicker and more capitalist to buy a jar of applesauce from the grocery store. But if you've ever bought prepackaged applesauce from a box store, you know full well that it is not free. And I am never one to turn down free food. That's how I ended up with the apples in the first place.

I pulled all the dishes out of the sink so that I could clean the apples. While they soaked, I made room for making applesauce by clearing overdue library books off the kitchen table and blowing away the dust. And then I spent the next three days peeling apples.

But when I was done, I had a heaping mound of apple scraps, and a notably smaller pile of chopped apples. I scooped these into a slow cooker. When they finished cooking down, I had my very own spoonful of applesauce. After all my effort, the applesauce was so delicious that I'll never do that again.

What matters most is that I did it once, and I crossed it off my list. My culinary success just goes to show that with a good to-do list, anything from Hollywood magic to frontier-style homesteading is possible. I hope this new get-things-done Congress is paying attention. If it can be twice or even three times as productive as I am, it is certain to accomplish as much as any Congress before it. And I hope Harrison Ford is around to see it.

The Secret's in the Stuffing

I HAVE A THANKSGIVING SECRET I need to spill. Like a stomachful of undercooked turkey, I can't hold it in even one second longer.

But first, I have to tell you about how I'm a vegetarian. I am a hardcore, diehard non-meat eater, at least for the moment. And I make no exceptions, except for a significant cross-cultural experience or when I want a hamburger.

I'm fortunate because my family stood by me when I declared my vegetarianism. They love me unconditionally and accept my dietary orientation as part of who I am, at least until Thanksgiving dinner.

As if the fourth Thursday in November is reserved for scarfing a bunch of food we otherwise never nibble, they all inquire if I'll be having turkey. After all, gobbling the gobbler is to being human what the dictionary is to words: it separates the Americans from the people who spell "color" with unnecessary vowels.

Sure, who doesn't love spicing up their green bean casserole with a few strips of bird flesh? I know I do. As a condiment for my all-plant diet, turkey comes second only to bacon's blue ribbon. But if I so much as let the turkey touch my taters, my family will doubt my otherwise devout meat-lessness the whole year through.

Thus, my deep dark-meat secret: I forgo turkey on Thanksgiving in order to remain a steadfast veggie man, even at the cost of my citizenship.

This freak show is about to go on the road. I'm having my first Thanksgiving at my prospective future in-laws' house. These borderland folks raised two wonderfully stubborn daughters and routinely fight off the neighborhood javelinas with a slingshot, yet my simple decision not to eat just one of the seventeen available dishes has turned meal preparation into a reality show.

Here's a sample of an actual telephone conversation I eavesdropped on completely by accident:

> **Prospective Future Mother-in-Law:** "What will Zach eat?"
> **Darling Fiancée:** "He'll eat whatever he wants."
> **PFMiL:** "But he doesn't eat meat."
> **DF:** "Then he'll pass on the turkey."
> **PFMiL:** "I need to make him something else. Can he eat ham?"
> **DF:** "..."

You may not believe me, but I truly don't miss turkey. The best parts of Thanksgiving dinner are made more possible by *not* eating turkey. These are: 3) sweet potatoes with marshmallows on top, 2) pumpkin pie, and 1) those hours in the late afternoon when everyone else is half unconscious on the couch and I can do anything I please in peace and quiet because I'm not all hopped up on the belief that tryptophan makes you sleepy.

And that's not all, muscle-munchers: being a vegetarian is stuffed with massive perks. For instance, carrots are cheaper than Omaha Steaks. I therefore save enough money to buy more beer, which doesn't contain meat, except when it does. (No matter how hard I try, I will never forget the oyster stout I ordered in a foreign pub once. It taught me that cross-cultural experiences, besides fostering international goodwill, can be really gross.)

But at least I didn't let the oyster stout go to waste, unlike a meaty craft beer I tried once in San Antonio. The brew tasted just like your traditional smokehouse wall, only with more carcinogens.

This is when being a vegetarian comes in handy. A normal human being feels guilty about sending a drink back to the bar, even when the drink tastes like a campfire extinguished the cowboy way. But a vegetarian can politely say, "I can't drink this beer because of the floating hoof bits," and the bartender throws out the vegetarian for this personal affront to carnivores everywhere, and the vegetarian doesn't have to pay for his salad and breadsticks.

Being a vegetarian on Thanksgiving also offers a chance to increase awareness of the conditions of meat farms in America today. Some folks read the Macy's ads in the newspaper every Thanksgiving; I read a short passage from the book *Eating Animals*, where author Jonathan Safran Foer discusses the potential joys of skipping the modern turkey—a factory-farmed animal as recognizable to the first brave pilgrims as a Velociraptor or Brad Pitt.

"Would the tradition be broken," he asks, "or injured, if instead of a bird we simply had the sweet potato casserole, homemade rolls, green beans with almonds, cranberry concoctions, yams, buttery mashed potatoes, pumpkin and pecan pies?

"Or would Thanksgiving be enhanced? Would the choice not to eat turkey be a more active way of celebrating how thankful we feel?"

I certainly think so. I for one celebrate not having to scrape the sack of frozen giblets from the turkey's body cavity. Mostly, though, I believe that Thanksgiving is all about celebrating our thankfulness for leftovers. So now that I've spilled my secret, my stomach and my conscience have plenty of room for turkey enchiladas.

No Taste
Like Home

THOSE OF US STILL ALIVE survived Thanksgiving, the busiest travel weekend of the year. Whew! But that doesn't mean we're done traveling. We're Americans, goldurnit, except for those of us who aren't. We go go go. And when you next leave town, how will you ensure that your pipes don't freeze and burst, or that your copper pipes don't get stolen, or that your lead pipe doesn't murder the butler in the conservatory?

Housesitters, that's how. These people—some of whom don't even look desperate—are willing to live in your home for about the price of a movie theater ticket per day, minus popcorn. But you can't trust just anyone to sleep in your bed, care for your pets, water your plants, tend to your garden, fend off your burglars, and eat your food. You need a reputable caretaker. That's why I'm coming out of retirement.

Actually, I'm coming out of retirement because an elderly neighbor is leaving town for a weekend. He's got a sweet house that's only about thirty percent sealed off like a mausoleum. It'll be like a weekend retreat in a Hitchcock film!

Some housesitting gigs really do offer peace, tranquility, and a back fridge fully stocked. But I won't bring those up here; though they are good for my soul, they are boring to talk about. Besides, the vast majority of housesitting assignments give sneak peeks into the private lives of other people, which is much more intriguing, because other people are insane.

(I must mention that I am a massive proponent of preserving privacy in one's own home. When homeowners invite me into their residences, they expect that I will honor their lives and personal space. I agree to do so, because they pay me money. Thus, I will change their identifying features while preserving every other detail to a T.)

To prove that other people are nuttier than a Planters-sponsored jock strap, you need look no further than their pets. Take, for instance, the dog who was afraid of houseflies. This story will kill you; I nearly died, but it all ended happily, and with Kevin Spacey. **[Editor's note: Unlike *House of Cards*, we could not afford to reshoot Mr. Spacey's role in this book. We apologize for his inclusion.]**

So this house was invaded by houseflies. Saturated. I was watching this house in the peak part of summer when every fly brought in by the state fair landed on whatever plate of food I scrounged together.

And "scrounge" is the right word. My clients always insist that I help myself to any food left in the house. Score! Free food helps balance out the pay.

Or it would, if I could stomach other peoples' tastes. There's a motto I've lived by ever since I just made it up: different tastes for different waists. And "tastes" range far beyond the culinary. For example, I once cared for a lovely straw bale house for nearly a month. The owners explained that a relative needed to use the house one evening for a company party, if I would please vamoose. No problem! I called the relative the day before the party to see if I could help prepare.

He asked me to clear my things out of the bathroom—not just the bathroom, but the shower.

"The guests are receiving towels as party favors," he explained, as if that cleared up everything.

I still do not know what kinky sex things occurred in that house, but I did not touch any surface for the rest of my stay. Especially the ghostly flour handprint smeared across the kitchen counter.

At first, I was a little freaked out. I've seen some things—one time, a wild predator ate a client's cat. But I had never hosted a corporate orgy.

Then I realized that I could imagine a perfectly reasonable explanation, such as: the office party bacchanal happened somewhere else, and then they all came to my temporary home to freshen up and eat sushi. I could accept that scenario.

Such mental flexibility has suited me well in my other bookings. It has also helped me become more accepting of those who are less normal than I am. I put myself in their shoes—sometimes literally—and contemplate what they would make of my wholesome American refrigerator, with its curry ketchup, its soy sauce, its Greek yogurt, and its corn tortillas. I realize that we are all citizens of the world, which means that—

Jinkies! I completely forgot to finish the story about the dog who was afraid of flies. I'll tell you that story another time, when I've run out of better ideas to talk about.

The Music Man

I HAVE LATELY BEEN PONDERING what it means to be a man. Manliness and manhood incorporate so many ideas of responsibility and strength, compassion and bodily odor, that it's difficult to bring a single all-encompassing idea into focus. But I recently came to the conclusion that being a man, more than anything else, means buying vinyl records.

This epiphany struck me—entirely coincidentally—when I went to the record swap at the local VFW. For weeks, I was anticipating the event not because it would lead me to enlightenment about my own masculinity, but because I was simply anxious to "comb through the stacks" and "hunt for wax" until I found that one record. The Holy Grail. The rare and elusive album I've been searching for my whole life, ever since I got back into vinyl this summer.

I didn't know what that album was, exactly, but I knew I would know it when I saw it, ya know?

"Get the good stuff before it's gone!" proclaimed the ads. Hot diggity, I was not going to miss out on meeting my One True Record. So when the big day came, I stuffed my cash in my pocket and got there in time to beat the crowds.

But the crowds had hit. Twenty, thirty people were already "flipping the hi-fis" when I strolled in. So I didn't deliberate. I pounced on the nearest table and dug into my quest.

Here's the thing with record swaps: the records already have owners, and these fellas like to talk with you. It's extremely difficult to evaluate whether or not each one of three thousand records is your vinyl soulmate when the vendor is busy telling you about how these records are from his own personal collection. They're so hard to part with, he says, because they're his prized possessions. He doesn't really want to part with them at all, as a matter of fact, but he has reasons.

He sizes you up at this point. Which reasons will get your sympathy and your cash? Maybe the wife says he has to sell them. Maybe he's just running out of room on his record shelves. Maybe he just feels bad hoarding triplicates of Dan Fogelberg's oeuvre.

It doesn't matter which story he tells me. I know I am in a position of power. If I don't personally buy all of these records, these vendors must schlep them back to their cars at the end of the day. And I know for a fact how heavy records are, because I have lost relatives by asking for their help on moving day.

So at the negotiating table, which happened to be the same table as the record-selling table, I had the high ground. I could have walked away, hands empty and pockets full. But that would have been a mistake, because there were so many good records to be had. Many for cheaper than a Taco Bell Gordita Supreme! And without the inevitable diarrhea, to boot.

I was not going to miss out on all this great music just because these records weren't my Holy Grail. So I traded little bits of my cash with the vendor here and there to buy some of his cherished "disco plates." Three measly dollars hardly dented my stash, no matter how many times I spent it.

I feel I must explain my use of "he" and "him" for the vendor. He was, to all appearances, a man. With only the rarest exception, all the vendors were male. And all the men elbowing me out of the way for Loretta Lynn discs were various shades of male.

This was a peculiar observation. Why don't more women attend record swaps and buy records? Does it have something to do with women having more sense than to spend actual money on an outdated and impractical form of recorded music? Or is it because—and I don't intend to generalize here—buying records is something only men do because it makes them manly and so by definition many women are excluded?

I think these questions would require greater thought, if it weren't so clear that buying records is a distinguishing feature of manhood. I feel good cradling this essential truth in my heart without further critical evaluation. Besides, even though I didn't find a single record that glowed under angelic spotlights and hummed with strains of Handel's *Messiah*, I'll be too absorbed by sitting at home and "tossing the licorice pizza" to do anything else. At least until I can afford groceries again.

Moolah Kalikimaka

YOU GUYS! I JUST GOT an *Angebot* I cannot possibly *verpass*! The email also said many other things in German, but the gist is that a kindly old woman wants to bequeath me six million euros. That's like Europe's version of Canadian dollars. And in return she wants ... nothing at all.

I feel like I'm living in a medley of Charles Dickens novels. I started out as Pip, the poor soot-covered orphan who couldn't even afford a real name. Now that I have a Generous Benefactress, I'm turning into Ebenezer Scrooge McDuck, a fabulously rich fellow whom everyone loves for his personality.

The Darling Fiancée assures me that this opportunity is a hoax. And if the message had come in some broken form of English, like it was written by a Nigerian kindergartener or a Canadian, I would believe her. But this is genuine! I know, because my Generous Benefactress must somehow have learned that I took German classes for two years in college. Which I did, and not only because it was not French. That is clearly part of the reason the GB chose me, of all the people in the world.

The Darling Fiancée thinks she has that all figured out, too. She claims that the German "spammer" found me because I once switched my Facebook language *auf Deutsch*.

Nuh uh! First of all, Facebook clearly and directly states that it will never allow outside parties to access users' information. Also, she is just plain wrong. I once set my Facebook language to Pirate, and no one has yet to offer me six million gold doubloons.

Long story short, this Christmas is going to be epic. For me, anyway. I understand not everyone has my formidable resources. That's why I'd like to relay some hard-earned wisdom, from when I too was poor, about how to enjoy the holidays anyway.

Think through Christmases past. Can you recall precisely what presents you found under the tree? (Or under the menorah? Or under the cross? Or under the stuffed moose head wearing a Santa cap? I want to include all belief systems here; I'm just not sure how you all celebrate Christmas.)

That is a trick question! I would never expect you to recall something as meaningful as a heartfelt gift. I can't even tell you what I ate for breakfast yesterday. Your loved ones will likewise forget your gifts to them. You can take advantage of this fact: during the holidays, what's inside doesn't count nearly as much as what's on the outside.

In other words, it's not the gift that matters, but the packaging.

As proof, I offer a true success story. When I was a kid, I gave my little sister a gift certificate because Steve Jobs or whoever had not yet invented gift cards. This was basically a sheet of paper that said, "Your brother loves you enough to spend five dollars on a sheet of paper, instead of just stuffing a bunch of nickels in an old M&M wrapper for you. You can buy anything you like! So long as this one specific store carries it for five dollars or less."

Some of us might find that gift pretty touching, but I knew my sister. She was the worst at quietly hiding her disappointment with gifts. (She has improved; now, she is the worst at *loudly* hiding her disappointment.) So to make the present memorable if not appreciated, I laid the gift certificate gingerly at the bottom of a big shipping box, and I filled the box with river rocks from somebody's yard.

This present was as heavy as a box full of river rocks. It sparked a whole month of speculation and wonderment. No one could conceive of something so heavy that I, with no legal access to a bulldozer, could procure.

When my sister finally got to the gift certificate, she was so overcome with Christmas joy that she cheered my full name and threw a river rock at me, in that loveable *you-shouldn't-have!* type of way.

Getting creative with your own ideas in this vein makes the holidays super affordable. For instance, if you live in Canada, you could forgive me for making fun of you twice in a single column. (Thrice, if you are a Canadian with a Christmas moose head.) Wherever you live, the spirit of my rock-solid wisdom is that you should always strive to make the holiday season more memorable for everyone, while making it cheaper for you.

And kids: if you are very lucky, and you study your foreign languages like Uncle Zach did, maybe, just maybe, you'll someday have your very own personal Frau Petra Krombacher von Lemke. But you'll have to wait until you're old enough to have a bank account, because even the most magical benefactress needs those routing digits.

Happy New Year?
Not So Fast

THE WINTER HOLIDAY SEASON has ended. Fir trees every-where are meeting their wood-chippers, and folks have drained all the nog and gobbled up all the figgy pudding. 'Tis the season now for resolving to burn off all the nog and pudding that stuck to our bones like staticky tinsel.

You see, this time of year truly asks us to become more complete people, to make our futures better than our pasts, and to grow as individuals and communities. And what better time to do so than when we are broke, stuffed, and overburdened with white elephant gifts?

To lend credence to this sociological theory, which I certainly did not just make up, I point to the indisputable historical fact that our modern New Year's Day might be possibly tied to the winter solstice, maybe.

The winter solstice marks the shortest day of the year. Ancient civilizations, such as the Chacoans, the Greeks, the Chinese, and hippies, all recognized the importance of this day to the annual cycle. By the solstice, all food had been harvested that wasn't devoured by chipmunks and bears, and every plant that couldn't survive the winter had died or dropped its leaves. The solstice was the time of death.

But the solstice also blocked out the schedule for revelry, drunken abandon, and mischief. For the rest of the friggin' year, everybody had to be, like, responsible and stuff, or else come winter they'd die, too. So why not take the time off and let their inner fools out to play?

Of course, every mess has a mother telling someone to clean it up. And so it was that the ancient peoples' mothers made them clean up after their solstice shenanigans and promise to be good kids the rest of the year.

So they resolved to grow more squash, or not to kill their neighbors' cattle when they (the cattle) (or, honestly, the neighbors) lowed all night long, or to build better hunting traps, or not to covet their friend's bootleg collection of Byrds concerts. They didn't arbitrarily assign these resolutions to the first of January. They incorporated their commitments into the cycle of the sun in the sky and the crops in the ground and the festival concert season. Failing to do (or not do) these tasks had real-world repercussions much more primal than not going to spin class.

In other words, they made these resolutions because their lives depended on it. They could literally die if they didn't figure out ways to live stronger and more wholesomely.

I am one of the few who preserve this do-or-actually-die mentality with resolutions. That's why my resolutions never fall off the treadmill before Martin Luther King, Jr. Day. My resolve is backed by more than a fresh set of calendar digits, which I'll write incorrectly on rent checks for half the year anyway. I don't need tangible, real-world phenomena for my new ab-busting and carb-cutting declarations to survive longer than grocery store poinsettias.

Unfortunately for me, I now have that real-world reason anyway, whether I want one or not. I'm too terrified to even look away from my resolutions this year, because I've discovered the Krampus.

Krampus, for the goody-goodies out there who haven't yet incurred its punishments, is an ancient KISS-tongued goat-demon from Europe who accompanies St. Nicholas and whips naughty children. The severely bad kids, it stuffs into its sack. Some say that Krampus devours those stolen children. My theory is that it condemns them to be live-audience members for *Dancing with the Stars*.

Whatever kind of wrath it divvies out like arsenic candy canes, this anti-Santee Claus embodies everything that mall Santas wish they could do with impunity to lap-wetting children.

You might suggest to me, "You're safe. No matter how immature you act all the time, Krampus won't mistake you for a child. You're too hairy."

To which I would answer that Krampus is older than all three Wise Men put together. It's even older than America. To a being that old, all of us mortals look like the Lollipop Guild.

Then you might say, "Krampus is made-up fun, and its current popularity is simply a response to contemporary disenchantment with the crass commercialization of the holidays. I mean, come on, even Charlie Brown would give up on his Christmas twig if he heard 'Jingle Bells' in September."

I agree with you, reader, that the only humane use of drone missiles is to obliterate any store that plays holiday tunes before Halloween. However, as much as I wish you were right about Krampus being made-up fun, you're wrong.

"Fine. But can we at least agree that you don't have to worry about Krampus until next December?" you ask. "It's the new year, a time of possibilities. Don't Krampus my style."

To which I say: "I am not at all envious of your terrible pun." That aside, Krampus is no mere seasonal bugaboo. Santa Claus might put the naughty-or-nice list on auto-pilot until December, but the Krampus never takes a vacay. It watches at all times; it's the do-or-die factor to living a better life (or living at all); and staving it off is the reason you should be good children who respect your resolutions.

You better make them meaningful resolutions, too—none of those cop-out obligations like "I resolve to eat more pizza." I'm talking a full-on, feed-the-world and love-thy-neighbor level of commitment. If you can make these resolutions last as long as a Christmas fruitcake, you too can manage to dodge an eternity of reality television for one more year.

No Admission

"No" is one of the most important words people learn as toddlers. It establishes boundaries, builds a sense of self, and enables one to sing the Bob Marley song "No Woman, No Cry." So I am pretty proud of myself for learning, finally, to just say NO when people ask me if I ski.

Not skiing is the blasphemy I've cradled ever since moving to Colorado. And I don't even have a deflector shield of handy excuses for not skiing. It's not because skiing is expensive and I don't have the gear (even though it is and I don't). I, quite simply, just don't *want* to ski. I don't want to learn. I don't want to try it, because I won't like it. And I'm tired of burying this part of myself under an avalanche of shame.

Around these parts, I could say something as unorthodox as "I'm part of Obama's secret menagerie," and the most severe response I might get is "Do you want another beer?" But for years I have repressed my entire lack of ski-lust, because other people get flayed with ski poles for admitting that they don't ski.

I've seen it happen. It's like a Choose Your Own Adventure novel:

Chapter 1: You are with a group of friends when one of them asks you, "Do you ski?" You sense that your entire future rests upon your answer. *If you lie and say yes, go to Chapter 2. If you say no, go to Chapter 4.*

Chapter 2: "What kind of skiing?" they ask in eerie unison. *If you mumble words that might sound like skiing terms, go to Chapter 3. If you stare blankly, go to Chapter 4.*

Chapter 3: "Come with us this weekend!" one of your friends says. "I have my old gear you can use if you need it, and if the kind of skiing you mumbled requires a lift ticket, my buddy will get you a discount." You are forced into a corner, and rather than actually go skiing and make a fool of yourself, you admit that you do not ski. *Go to Chapter 4.*

Chapter 4: Your so-called friends gape at you. "You don't?" they say. "Surely you must be mistaken. Everyone skis." *If you decide to backpedal, go to Chapter 2. If you decide to fake a serious ski-related injury, go to Chapter 5. If you stick to your guns, go to Chapter 6.*

Chapter 5: Your friends offer you sympathy over your trashed ACL and suggest you go skiing together next winter. You have averted disaster for another year. THE END.

Chapter 6: The pack of your former friends closes tightly around you. The light dims, and you welcome the inevitable onslaught. At least, in death, you will never again have to answer questions about skiing. THE END.

This year, I am finished with choosing the same old adventures. I'm writing a new chapter, where I declare unabashedly that I CHOOSE NOT TO SKI and I will have tons of fun without paying for the privilege of breaking my femurs.

Holy powder days, what a liberating sensation this is. I'm going to make an entire lists of all sorts of other things I'm supposed to like that I don't! You ready for this? I don't like New Year's Eve. I don't like the NFL. I don't like that I don't understand what the hell a "tapas" is. And I'm discovering right now that I really dislike making lists.

However, as many toddlers learn by the time they're thirty or forty, "no" is way more powerful when it is coupled with the power of "yes." Saying *nein* frees me to be loud and proud about also saying *ja*. If I am crystal clear about both what I like and what I don't like, then I will live life true to myself, even if I lose my remaining acquaintances.

So what do I like? That is an excellent question, one I intend to spend much of the next year exploring. There must be lots of things in the world to enjoy beyond not skiing. Like not snowboarding, for instance. But for the present, it turns out I really, really enjoy just saying no to things.

So come on. Make my day. Ask me to ski, please, so I can turn you down. And if you don't like my answer, then ask me again. Because I might give cross country a shot.

Bench
Oppressed

I GUARANTEE THAT I AM WAY AHEAD of everyone else's New Year's resolutions. Check that box, notch that belt, color me successful—we're just skidding into January, and I have already outgrown my naïve resolution to exercise at the gym.

I should mention that I already owned the killerest biceps of the entire English Department Class of 2007 at my alma mater, so far as I could tell through the graduation gowns. And unlike my peers who went on to earn doctorates and professorships, I let neither my body nor my mind slip.

With that advantageous head start, I have set lofty new goals to buff up even more muscles. For instance, I estimate that I can reach five full sit-ups by the end of ~~the next Clinton~~ the Oprah administration.

Yet my primary motivation in going to the gym was never about "trimming down" or "gettin' swol." I went to enjoy the dedicated me-time. I yearned to escape the hustle and bustle of hiking trails and fresh air by popping in some ear buds and looking really athletic for fifteen minutes.

But—and you dudes out there will understand precisely what I'm talking about—it's *impossible* to go to the gym without being ogled all the time. The feeling of eyeballs scouring your physique grows even harsher when you walk out of the locker room wearing Spandex shorts.

The discomfort starts the moment I enter the building. The counter attendant—a different counter attendant both times, I'll have you know—stalks me all the way to the check-in computer. She lingers there with my temporary membership card. Then, offhandedly, as casually as she might suggest closing an umbrella indoors, she asks me if I'd like a towel. Oh ho! I would get smacked for so much as *mentioning* a piece of terrycloth drying sweat from *her* unmentionables, if I'd ever had the thought, which I certainly didn't. But as a man at the gym, this kind of abuse is simply to be endured.

The blatant leering worsens in the actual fitness area. A woman who thinks she's God's gift to men always lingers behind me. She justifies her hovering examination of my posterior by asking if the drinking fountain will be available soon, even though I'm clearly flushing all the germs out of the mouthpiece before I drink. Ms. God's-Gift could use a little less time on the lat pulldown and a little more time on sensitivity training, if you ask me. Instead, I'm supposed to accept her undesired advances as a compliment.

It never stops. Women inquiring if the spin bike is free, or if I am just warming up the saddle. Women grazing me on the indoor track as I dash onto it. Women wiping up my sweat when I'm finished with the leg press. And just when I think I'm home free, the counter attendant lasciviously begs me to come back again soon.

Really, the only escape from this onslaught of sexual oppression is the locker room. We men stand united in our sanctuary. Here, we can talk to total strangers about what we lift, yes, but also about our deepest worries: what's happening at home, whether our kids will be okay through the divorce, how good those counter attendants must be in the sack.

Rather, I should say that Other Men have these conversations in the locker room. I mostly try to keep my gaze averted, because Other Men feel it's perfectly acceptable to commune with each other in complete nakedness, without so much as a flip flop.

It is standard, documented etiquette that any two given men may not so much as whisper about sports and cars while standing shoulder to shoulder at the urinals. Yet somehow a handshake with full-frontal nudity is a-okay? There's a Nobel prize for the crack scientist who riddles out that phenomenon.

As for my own incidental observations, I've now paired every single concern I have about aging with visual confirmation. I also know precisely how I size up to your average sixty-something gym member in the, well, "gym member" department. But that's not what bugs me most. What really bugs me is that a bunch of athletes are walking around in their bare feet. What do you get when you mix athletes and sweaty feet?

Sopping wet floors, that's what! Also, this behavior can spread some form of toe fungus, but I can't remember its common name right now so I'll skip that point and go right back to aggressive attention from brazen women.

You may think I should feel flattered. But there's more to me than skin and muscles. I've moved on from the gym because I want to be respected—nay, revered!—for my more deeply-rooted qualities. For instance, I still have some hair. It's up here, if you can pry your imagination off my Lycra.

A Hard–Baked Case

THE WORLD IS CHANGING, FOLKS. Used to be, we worked our minimum wage jobs and we went home happy to have employment and we didn't say peep about nothing going on in the world. But nowadays, progressive burghs like Los Angeles are bringing about the end days by paying a so-called "living" wage. Illicit drugs are turning legal. And soccer is becoming America's pastime.

These changes are the reasons we need a defender. I am not that defender. But I do own a fedora. So I will go under-cover to uncover what is behind these nefarious plots to ruin good citizens like myself.

That's right. I'm a private columnist patrolling the mean streets. But not in Los Angeles. I can't stand traffic. And not anywhere with a soccer team, because the offside rule makes no sense. Instead, I will venture into the seedy underbelly of the Colorado dope syndicate.

I have lived in Colorado since before the dawn of retail marijuana. As an inside observer, I have dutifully noted how every aspect of society has changed not one whit. Except that weed now comes with itemized receipts.

All this not-changing is not something I, a hardboiled columnist, can write about. Time to find out what's really going on. I'll be a tough guy, I will. I won't even ask the tough questions—I'll just demand the tough answers. I will scrape to the bottom of all that is rotten with this world so you don't have to.

It might get rough. It might get tumble. I might need backup. So I am bringing my dad.

Pops is tough. In a pinch, he can run away really fast. But he might need additional backup. So he is bringing his friend, too.

And this friend is *really* tough. I personally witnessed this friend ride a bicycle up a mountain without Gatorade. Let's call him "Studs McGuffin," because his wife doesn't know half the things he does and I won't be the one to get him busted.

We three cased a local marijuana dispensary. The inside was camouflaged like the lobby of a particularly posh hotel. But I know better than to be fooled by a pretty façade. This front was masking some flop house or Grateful Dead shrine. I felt it.

We surrendered our driver's licenses at the front counter and were ushered to our own private shopping experience. Behind the door, this place was gussied up with fine wood paneling, glass countertops, and tasteful lighting. A young man introduced himself as our "budtender." He shuffled display jars of whole-flower marijuana. What deceptive little plants these were. Satan Incarnate, according to the D.A.R.E. crossword puzzles I solved in fifth grade, yet as unassuming as dumplings.

The selection was a bit overwhelming to certain members of our party. Fortunately, none of us could actually buy anything. Pops is an employee of the federal government with a high-level security clearance that authorizes him to visit the restroom without supervision. Studs does not partake, in case his wife finds out who I mean when I say "Studs." And I am an objective fly-on-the-wall reporter, which means I have no money.

But that didn't stop me from applying my stranglehold interrogation tactics. I demanded tough answers to every question Pops asked.

POPS: "Where do you grow all this?"
BUDTENDER: "It's all Colorado grown. I'm not able to tell you the exact location of our grow, though, for security purposes."
ME: *[cants fedora at an even more skeptical angle]*
STUDS: "Duuuuuude! Check out all this great stuff!"

I refused to let this slippery employee wriggle away from all the facts. So when my lean-n-mean stares failed to reel in tough answers, I dropped my own choice lingo that I picked up by reading labels in the display case. "What's the sativa CBD of your chocolate hybrid glassware contents?" I demanded.

"Well, CBD is often an excellent aid in reducing pain and inflammation without the psychoactive effects of THC," the budtender said, cloaking his answer in so much ignorance that I knew he must be just a low-level lackey in the ganja syndicate.

That's when it struck me. Peddling marijuana is just like peddling pints, or peddling pizza, or peddling anything else at wages marginally acceptable only to tongue-chewing young adults. The kids "tending" these "buds" aren't connected to anyone "in the know." They're just making a buck. And their employers are here to stay. Because nothing, not even middling customer service or crack investigative columnists, can stop people from buying the things they love most.

America may not be in good hands, but it's at least in the same low-level lackey hands that brought it this far. And those hands deserve a respectable wage, considering how much stuff Studs McGuffin is totally not buying from them.

Off
the Charts

Until you *really* master social media, #keepingtabs-onyourfavoritecelebrityistough. #igetit. That's why you, my dedicated readers, deserve to hear it straight from me, with normal punctuation and spaces: I am a rock star.

You have likely not heard my greatest hits yet. That's only because I'm not a mediocre rock star, selling out to any worthy cause with a benefit show. But I have all three primary qualifications for being a GREAT rock star:

1. I own a guitar.
2. I can make very loud noises using my throat.
3. I have principles, dammit, and those principles bend for no corporation unless it offers me a bunch of money.

At least those were the qualifications for being great in the days of Nirvana, The Beatles, and Mozart. The blueprint was flexible; a band lacking one or even all of those requirements found other routes to success.

For instance, any ol' unfortunate incident involving a helpless mammal, like a bat or a shark, convinced parents and other squares that the band worshipped the devil. This, in turn, cemented an entire generation of devoted teenagers who, over the course of their lives, would buy the vinyl, the eight-track, the cassette, the CD, the MP3, and the remastered 180-gram vinyl reissue of every album.

But there's sadly no such golden ticket to success in today's shrinking field of rock-stardom. More shocking things happen every week on reality shows like *Pawn Stars*, where people haggle over the remains of both the bat and the shark. (The most shocking bit is how much the seller thinks they are worth, despite lacking Certificates of Authenticity.)

A common crapshoot tactic for today's would-be rock stars is to film videos in their backyards. Because music is a visual art form, the most successful backyards have irrationally attractive people jiggling about them, preferably on trampolines or diving boards.

Bands post these videos on YouTube, a highly selective online media filter. Hitting it big on YouTube is simple because every video instantly receives eighty-three million page views like *that*. This built-in audience guarantees a certain demographic—scientifically categorized as "old people"—impulsive enough to click on the ads, thereby generating revenue for the band members' girlfriends.

If modern musicians want to branch out and play actual gigs, however, they are expected to tune their own instruments, schlep their own amplifiers, drive their own vans, and fend off their own crazed groupies. This is *way* too much work for true-rooted rockers like me. Work is for The Man, as well as for roadies. That's why, nowadays, the surest way to the top is to win a contest.

Contests work exactly like democratic republics, except people actually vote in contests because they can use smartphones. However, *great* rock stars never enter traditional televised music contests. We don't believe that a single vowel should contain thirty-seven syllables and imitate an elk's last desperate mating call.

So imagine my delight over National Public Radio's Tiny Desk Concert Contest.

(Lingo check: Tiny Desk Concerts are, quite clearly, concerts given around a tiny desk. Or else they are tiny concerts performed around a normal-sized desk. And radios are science-fiction devices able to transmit song waves without the aid of the internet. Someday, they will be installed in every flying car.)

Tragically, this entry period has ended. You are spared having to compete with me. I'm a shoo-in, because I already own a desk. Furthermore, entrants must write their own songs. I already wrote this chapter. How much harder could writing one measly culture-defining song be?

The answer: not even a tiny bit harder. Songs generally have fewer words than a Scooby-Doo Valentine card, and they are less intelligible. Seriously—does *anybody* know what Elton John sings after the line "Goodbye, yellow brick road"? Where the dug one inside of me hounds? You can't catch me in a vent now? I'm boating back to my clown?

I can't disclose the secret lyrics of my award-winning song here without causing another stampede. But stay tuned to the top o' the charts! I'll wave at you from way up there.

UPDATE: Okay, so writing a song isn't all it's cracked up to be. It's much more boring. And a lot fewer words rhyme with "sexy grapefruit" than you might expect.

I'm not frittering away my life on lyrics when everyone knows it's the rhythm guitarist who defines all great Rock and Roll Hall of Fame inductees. Speaking of which, how many chords should a rock idol learn before imploding? I hope less than two, since I'm still looking into what exactly a chord is, anyway.

For Immediate Press Release

I WOULD LIKE TO ANNOUNCE—and I may be alone here—that I am not running for president.

It's not that I don't have vision. I was once deemed legally sighted when I had my eyes checked. And it's not that I have a problem with gathering unlimited quantities of corporate free speech for my campaign. Get while the gettin' is constitutional, I say. No, I elect to remain unelected because of social media.

Every candidate has social media these days. Candidates love to interact candidly with their campaign staff, who then draft tweets for focus groups and media consultants, whose feedback modifies the tweet until it says nothing whatsoever. Only at this point does the staff release it to the general public. **[Editor's note: Seriously. This used to be actually, really truly, the way it worked.]**

This sort of spontaneous interaction is designed to woo the tech-fluent demographics. And it works great! Except for the one teensy flaw that every presidential candidate must be, in accordance with the Missouri Compromise, at least thirty-five years old. This means that no legal presidential contender today can find where they saved their sticky note of passwords.

You think I'm exaggerating. Let's look at entirely random historical examples of technological aptitude. Republican Senator Ted Cruz, since at least 2016, has not owned the domain tedcruz.com. As of press time, the site is a template offering unspecified services. And Hillary Clinton, a leftish blue-state candidate, embodied her otherwise legitimate campaign with a graphic featuring a red arrow pointing right. This logo also utilized all the design capabilities of the Apollo 11 lunar shuttle.

These, cherished readers, are the sorts of people who want to run the free world and lord it over the less-free parts. This would be my competition if Congress reconsidered that thirty-five-year rule. **[Editor's note: Thirty-five snuck up on you faster than you thought, huh?]** But at any age I would still choose not to run because I have, and more relevantly I have had in the past, personal social media accounts.

You see, these accounts were not filtered by campaign strategists. They were not even filtered by my own judgment of what my grandparents ought not to see, let alone prospective constituents. And even though I am always and entirely innocent in my online activity, other people's posts never fail to catch me in seemingly compromising positions.

In fact, because of other people's posts, I'm quite certain that in a few years no one will be electable ever. And thank goodness! Because I'm already exhausted by the next presidential election taking place in ... carry the seven ... drop the four ... count the boxes ... *ALREADY?*

That's it! I cannot simply watch as pre-presidential politics result in another half decade of television commercials recorded with Boeing-quality decibels. It's time I become engaged in the political process by focusing even more of my energies on revamping my social media presence.

This step is not even writerly procrastination. I am a modern writer, and modern writers build platforms. It's rather a lot like how the U.S. Forest Service builds roads. It all makes a lot of sense, once you stop thinking about it.

I could pretty much build a social media empire with my eyes closed. After all, I have deep secondhand knowledge of what an Instagram is, and how it differs from a LinkedIn. The only thing stopping me is that, as a modern writer building a platform, I don't have time to dither with social media. That's why I had my little sister set up my Tumblr account.

Tumblr, for the uninitiated, is not quite a Pinterest, and it's definitely not a TikTok. I made a savvy move in having Kara post in my place, because she is the youth vote, and her own unaltered words were, "I am determining that Tumblr is a scary place, just based on the list of suggested usernames it tried to give me."

I can't make this stuff up, because you readers expect the guise of honesty. So I will transcribe the text messages my sister machine-gunned me:

> *Let's see I just started to set up an account and got*
> *Chocolate Student Goatee. Lovely Spooky Donut.*
> *The other ones were worse. These are a lot, better?*
> *Speedily Fancy Poetry. Zealous Taco Tragedy. Sweetly*
>   *Furry Triumph.*
> *You could do this all day.*
> *Too Nut Basement. Dope Kitten Galaxy.*
> *Zealous Fart Typhoon. Always Salty Time Machine.*
> *I am going to keep texting until you respond.*
> *Just kidding I need to do homework. But I am thinking*
>   *about changing you to the Zealous Fart Typhoon.*

Does any one of our current prospective presidents have the moxy to handle a zealous taco tragedy? The savvy to spin an always salty time machine into a *sometimes* salty time machine? I guarantee they do not!

Yet the candidates get away with dodging the issues, because they can build their platforms by selling dinner tickets at fifty thousand dollars a plate. So in exchange for your contribution, I, as President Fart Typhoon, promise not to post your most unflattering pictures. Even if I remember where I saved them.

Lights Out

I HAVE TRACED MY ANCESTRY as far back as Paleolithic cave-men and rural West Virginians. Yet I never understood their rough subsistence—not fully—until my power went out.

So I didn't have electricity. Big deal, right? We humans shape the world with the mere strength of our minds. Climate change does not exist, so long as we refuse to acknowledge it. Borders, governments, religions, and the success of ABBA could not endure without our constant and combined mental fortitude. A little loss of electricity should hardly matter to such a superior being as I.

And it didn't, for a half hour or so. I played FreeCell in actual peace and quiet, without the refrigerator complaining and the neighbor's television murmuring. Then the un-thinkable happened, and it was more unsettling than any blizzard-induced Whole Foods riot:

My laptop battery died.

I plugged it in. Nothing. I flipped the switch on my surge protector. Nothing. Odd, as the old turn-it-off-and-back-on-again school of IT repair never failed me before.

I could not allow this predicament to conquer me. I am a rational being. So I did what any manly American male would do in such a situation; namely, I flipped the light switch in every room I entered—completely on purpose, mind you, just to see if the problem was isolated in an ungrounded oscillating fuse transmission cable box router, which sounded likely enough.

But no matter how many rooms I wandered through, I still could not find a flashlight. The gravity of this situation finally weighed on me about as much as normal gravity: if the lights didn't work, then the microwave might not work either. I could very reasonably starve to death in the time it took me to cook a can of beans on the stovetop.

For the first time since my little sisters pooled their allowances to buy a brand-new Spice Girls CD, I panicked. I needed to find the answers, and I needed to find them *RIGHT NOW*.

So I went to look up "how to survive a power outage" on the internet. I pounded the computer power button five or six times and promptly realized I was an idiot. You see where this is going, right? The internet could not save me. It is nothing but a rabbit hole of "37 Reasons You Broke Up With Your Ex, Explained By Eighties Movie Soundtracks." It would not contain the answers I sought.

Actual useful information, on the other hand, was stored in books before they went extinct. Fortunately, I own enough books to make me look smart. That trick finally paid off! But if I wanted to stay awake while reading the manual on surviving the end of the world as I knew it, I required a cup of coffee. I pulled out my coffee grinder, poured in the beans, pressed the button, and discovered that my electric coffee grinder runs on none other than ... electricity.

(It's obvious to me *now*, smarty-pants, but people like me attempting to function under duress are precisely why electronics companies ought to add one more line to the warning tag; e.g., DOES NOT FUNCTION DURING POWER OUTAGES OR IN RURAL WEST VIRGINIA.)

The scene was not pretty. All I can say is, thank goodness I'm not one of those people addicted to coffee, or else I might have really lost my cool when I went to boil water to brew some whole-bean coffee and discovered that the ignitor on a gas range also runs on none other than electricity, and I needed actual matches to light the flame, only I didn't *have* any matches because for *months* the grocery store has stocked only the foot-long variety, which I felt ridiculous buying in bulk.

After timeless hours of anxiety, despair, and fetal-positioning in an unheated corner until my eyelashes froze together, I shifted my paradigm. I decided to look forward to "roughing it"—camping out in the living room; reading a good old-fashioned data-packed book by lantern light; guzzling room-temperature cocoa, ideally before the milk curdled in the dead refrigerator. Heck, I would do so every night for a week, and it would be kinda fun, until I had to resort to eating toothpaste.

I hoisted myself up by my hillbilly bootstraps and relied for some time on my primitive ancestry. First task: get warm. No fire? Must find thick furs. Thick fur nice. Warm. Grrnh.

Zach still hunt for dead animal skin when cloud-fire flash! Hear growl, whir, hum, strange birds. Saber-tooth? No. This hurt eyes and ears. Too much strange fire!

Only ... only better than fire. White light not burn hand. Must make words for new strange power. Call it, Just In Time For Lunch.

Tipping Point

Welcome to the Fool's Gold Advice Column for Smarties. It's just like "Dear Abby," only richer with expletives.

This week, our topic is: TIPPING.

Tipping is the act of giving money to the waitstaff at a restaurant so that their hornswaggling bosses don't have to. Tipping perplexes many otherwise intelligent diners, possibly because it involves calculating percentages on a full stomach. So how can you know, quickly and reliably, how much to tip your server?

Answer: Always tip generously, unless you're a complete chumbucket.

Well ... that's that. It turns out that tipping is not as difficult as scurvy bilge rats make it out to be. So let's go on to talk about something else that annoys me.

Please allow me to start off by saying that I like the United States Postal Service. It is a venerable institution that preserves the endangered tradition of people mailing bona fide handwritten checks for my birthday. I also acknowledge the positive economic impact the USPS has on my community by hiring no fewer than two (2) employees to serve the entire county.

I do not—cannot!—fault either of these fine employees for my hardships at the post office, because I've never met them. In fact, I am starting to suspect that, unless I cut in line like a slack-sailed deck swabber, I will never actually reach them to mail my Christmas packages.

No, I'm not some dimwitted laggard who forgot to mail his Christmas presents in time. Rather, I shrewdly and pro-actively avoided the entire postal service in December, when the local office sometimes hires a third landlubber to give the impression that the line will move more quickly, or at all. But we Smarties—this includes you, so long as you're reading this Advice Column for Smarties—know better. During the holiday season, defined by the USPS as "any calendar year with a holiday in it," the post office has the longest and most restless line I have ever seen. And I once worked as a bookseller for the midnight release of a Harry Potter novel.

So here we are in February, and I still have all these pirate insult dictionaries to ship to my dearest relations, and the sorry sea dogs will have to wait Davy Jones knows how long to enjoy them.

The Postal Service is falling apart, matey. First to dance the hempen jig were the lickable stamps. Future generations will never comprehend that strange tacky taste of glue. Now it's the ability to mail packages online without camping outside the PO like I'm buying Coachella tickets. Next thing you know, neither of the postal workers will be driving the classic white breadboxes with the steering wheel on the wrong side. That's because, in all seriousness, they (the trucks, but also the employees) were built to handle carrying letters, not to survive Prime shipping.

The peculiar thing is, not everyone gets the shaft like I do. *Someone* is mailing bulky items, because the USPS has seen a boost in holiday packages. I'd like to know if any of those were sent by regular Americans, or whether the Large Online Retailers finally overwhelmed and elbowed out all the grandmothers trying to send presents to their beloved grandsons, the worm-riddled blaggards. (The Large Online Retailers, I mean. Not the grandsons, and certainly not the grandmothers, mostly.)

Meanwhile, the Postal Service thinks it can keep jacking up our rates while extending delivery times. Talk about hoisting us over the yardarm! Doesn't the Postmaster General realize that for less than fifty cents I can practically deliver a letter to rural Montana my own grog-snarfing self? And since the United States has yet to democratize any other solar systems, what do we need universal service for, anyway?

Nothing, that's what! Yet those of us who suck at tax evasion dump billions of dollars into a government bureaucracy that doesn't like to work on Saturdays and thinks of us as Current Residents rather than as individuals.

Hang on a tick—I've confused the Postal Service with Congress. No doubt because both my local mail workers deliver so many informative political flyers to my mailbox every election season. At first I was flattered at the attention from my prospective representatives, but then I realized the pox-faced freebooters were two-timing me, sending identical notes to all my neighboring Current Residents.

Maybe the Postal Service is not the mutinous pack of salt swillers I thought it was. Perhaps it requires a bit more tender love to stay afloat, just like the other romantic anachronisms that still define our great nation—things like trains, chivalry, national parks, and Hotmail.

These institutions all deserve serious, considered preservation, except for Hotmail. That's why Congress should consider tossing a few extra doubloons at the United States Postal Service as a hearty thank-ye-kindly for decades of schlepping glossy campaign junk mail. I suggest they chip in at least twenty percent, the hook-handed swabs.

A Love–Hat
Relationship

I RECENTLY TREATED THE DARLING FIANCÉE to a staging of *Chicago*, the classic and ever-popular musical about a scrappy young woman rising above the law to make many new friends. The evening had everything a girl wants: friendship, love, danger, well-coordinated outfits, a rousing finale.

Oh, and *Chicago* was pretty good, too.

A gentleman never discloses the details. But mere gentlemen don't pull off date nights like I do—so I am spilling. Hear ye, all people (gentle or otherwise) interested in wooing a woman; this is my recipe for how to roll:

> **Vacuum the dust off your best sports jacket and wear it.** Be sure to check the pockets. If they still contain ticket stubs from the last show you went to, springboard into a nostalgic reminiscence with your lady. This is sure to spark deep affections and remembrances, unless it turns out you went to that show with your last girlfriend, which explains why your lady doesn't remember ever seeing your sports jacket before.

Invite two of your lady's dearest friends to a preshow dinner. Casually drop into the conversation that this is your anniversary celebration, even though it isn't. Her friends will feel honored to pay! This inclusion of friends is more than just considerate; it's morally obligatory, like waiting until your lady is off powdering her nose again to inform the waiter that today is her birthday, so that you get free ice cream and the restaurant gets a tax write-off.

Use the dinner and dessert savings to pay off the credit card you used to buy tickets to your lady's favorite musical production, *even if*, **for the same price, you could have bought her the DVD, the soundtrack with the original Broadway cast, and a plane ticket to the actual city of Chicago.** This is a good idea *EVEN IF* you and everyone else already know by heart the story of Roxy what's-her-face inspiring a bunch of imprisoned inner-city girls through the restorative powers of dance and lies under oath.

Now, those EVEN IF points are real stickers. If you're the kind of person interested in wooing a woman, strong odds you are also the kind of person who knows that musical theater is a racket for milking money out of those select few demographics who believe—often vehemently—that real-life people ought to break out in song and dance.

Just because *she* enjoys ensemble numbers more than cinematic explosions, why should *you* have to suffer through two whole acts and an intermission in the kind of theater that doesn't even sell popcorn?

I can't help you there. But I understand your plight. I too grew up scarred by sisters ceaselessly watching *The Sound of Music*. But I'm here to tell you that *Chicago* is so much more than a musical. Whatever your proclivities, you'll notice that the live show contains dozens of the fittest young dancers bending and arcing and spreading and shimmying every which way in next to no clothing, which really draws your attention to their very fine hats.

I love hats. Fedoras, bowlers, trilbies, Panamas, pork pies. I love wearing them, I love trying them on, I love tipping them at a rakish angle over my brow. I hate shopping, yet I would shop for hats until the cows come home. (I don't own cows, so that will be a very long time, indeed.) Yet the objective nature of professional journalism prevents me from expressing my personal thoughts about stylish hats. It's not fair that you, my most dedicated readers, still have no idea how I feel about them.

Wearing a hat in public in the United States of America is impossible nowadays if you care to follow proper hat etiquette. For instance, no restaurant provides a hat check or even a hat rack. I'm supposed to, what, hang my hat on the ketchup bottle? Not likely—where I dine, Heinz comes in packets.

It's also not Heinz anymore; I don't know what brand it is, but it says "fancy" on the package. And in the days of yore that *Chicago* portrays with historical impeccability, any fancy restaurant worth its condiments employed a maître d' ready to take your hat and pilfer your coat pockets.

In the immortal lyrics of Mama and that other unforgettable character whom everyone loves, Thelma or Valerie or something, whatever happened to class?

I know precisely what happened to class. But after admiring the real class acts in *Chicago*, I'm going to try gentlemanliness on for size. And a gentleman never tells.

Finally, something I can hang my hat on.

All Gut,
No Glory

I AM IMMOVABLY SICK with a malaise unrecognized by modern medicine. And I am not alone. Half the world's population is distressed with the same invisible poison, and it's not radon or whatever gas you get when you mix bleach and ammonia. No, it's much more serious. I—*deep breath, Hively. You can do this.* I—I am a man.

This is a huge problem. Because for all the opportunity in the world today, all we men have left to aspire to is the dad bod.

The term "dad bod" is not new, but the affliction is even older—as old as fermented barley water. If you have not yet been introduced to the dad bod, find the man nearest to you right now. That man has a dad bod, unless you are reading this at the Abercrombie store on Fifth Avenue, whose door wardens are more chiseled than the stone lions at the New York Public Library.

The dad bod body type is exemplified by dads, who frequently have trouble shedding those few extra pounds they added during the pregnancy. But a man doesn't have to carry a child to end up with a dad bod. Pretty much every grown male willing to take his shirt off at a public swimming pool has one.

Remember in elementary school, when our teachers told us that if we worked hard and memorized our multiplication tables and stopped chewing gum in class, we could become anything we wanted to be when we grew up? They lied. At least to us boys. Anything worth accomplishing, a man has already accomplished. I could never be the first man to walk on the moon, the first male president, or the guy in the Dos Equis commercials.

The dad bod exemplifies this stasis. Nothing special is possible anymore. Sure, I can win a Pulitzer or invent something nifty, but whatever. Even Nobel laureate Ernest Hemingway and former President George Herbert Walker Bush never amounted to anything more impressive than a dad bod. We guys are what we are.

Women, on the other hand, have entire universes of potential. They are still free to become the first anything! The sky, as clear as glass, is their limit. They don't have a dad bod capping their potential—everywhere you go, advertisements and television shows and magazines depict the attainable feminine ideal, with toned abs and flawless skin and enough beauty products to turn any ol' frump into a woman deserving of umlauts in her name.

Women, in other words, have something to strive for. They have goals to get them out of bed in the morning. They can get back in bed that night knowing they strode a step closer to perfection.

Even if women don't want to be political leaders or attractive, they still get to be superheroes. They have the freedom to work multiple jobs for less pay than us salary-locked dudes. They attend school functions for children they are free to birth or not—their choice! at least in some places!—and earn higher degrees while volunteering for the Red Cross, riveting rivets, and baking lasagna from scratch for their significant others, regardless of their significant others' body types.

And don't even get me started on clothing. Today's fashions epitomize our culture's gender inequity. Women can choose almost literally anything to wear. A woman can attend an exclusive gala wearing nothing but the plastic rings from six-packs, and this is a valid fashion decision. Women select their attire from infinite combinations of jackets, jewelry accessories, blouses, tops, scarves, footwear, hairstyles, hair accessories, belts, sequins, buttons, buckles, brooches, corsages, glasses, monocles, and an incomprehensible range of undergarments.

Men? Pants. Shoes. Shirt. Jacket. To top it all off, a tie. You might as well require us to wear a dog collar. We can't ever wear a skirt instead of pants, not even if we want to, unless we want everyone to know we are pretending to be more Celtic than we are.

For a fleeting moment, back when college sophomore Mackenzie Pearson published the first celebration of the dad bod in *Odyssey*, she assured me and all men that our body types and lifestyle choices were valid and beautiful in the eyes of a nineteen-year-old coed. But then some of these men—not pointing fingers at myself here—flexed in front of the bathroom mirror and went right back to feeling like garden slugs.

Still, it was a small victory. We have a long uphill slog until men reach true equality. I dream of a day when, if we are very lucky and very apathetic, the world will accept men of all shapes and motivations as worthy, legitimate, and hairy human beings.

The Toastest
with the Mostest

MY ELDEST LITTLE SISTER recently announced her engagement. She then quickly announced her wedding date, shortly pursued by the wedding itself. The whole process didn't leave a lot of room for your classic wedding traditions, like bridal showers or planning an actual ceremony.

This arrangement was perfectly fine by me. As a dude of the male gender, my philosophy regarding family weddings is to stay out of the way beforehand, show up looking mighty fine or at least better than my dad, and leave before it's time to clean up the aftermath. Being the only son—and the oldest offspring—in a gaggle of sisters, there was plenty of girl-enthusiasm to take up any slack.

But about six days before The Day, the bride tested my dedicated lack of involvement. That's when she—let's call her "Mrs. Pain," because that is phonetically the same as her new name—bestowed me with a Wedding Responsibility. She asked me to give a toast.

Now don't get me wrong—of all the Responsibilities being doled out in Mrs. Pain's waning days of spinsterhood, giving a toast was the one for me. I may not be the *numero uno* choice for finding a caterer, or booking a photographer, or bearing the rings, or planning a bachelor party, or keeping quiet during the rehearsal. But I sure know how to whip up a piece of writing on short notice.

Crafting the perfect toast would be a piece of wedding cake. All I really had to do was figure out what I wanted to say about my sister—something deeply meaningful and heartfelt, while at the same time sincerely mortifying. And what I wanted to say about her fiancé, Mr. Pain, whom I had met only once, while he had altitude sickness and too much New Mexico green chile in his Tennessee belly. And about weddings and marriages in general, despite being myself neither wedded nor married. And keep it quick and punchy, all while discovering a unifying theme to hold the whole thing together.

All those tasks are what I do best. So I did the other thing I do best: I opened myself to receive true inspiration whenever it struck. I know better than to rush the magic. So I did not even put pen to paper, lest I frighten off the skittish muses.

I stayed wide open during the drive to Albuquerque for the event. I remained receptive while all my other sisters' boyfriends worked to prepare the venue, leaving Pops and me free to take a long bike ride, far far away. I made myself an empty vessel for bright ideas while taking the soon-to-be-Pains-in-law out for beers.

By bedtime the night before the wedding, I knew I was on the right track. I had a beginning. It went like this:

"I'd like to propose a toast."

Classy. Solid. Nothing elaborate or intricate. My audience would know precisely the purpose of my oration, which is an outcome they probably teach you in public speaking classes.

I brushed my teeth, mulling over second lines. I texted our sister Kara to see if maybe the muses had mistakenly visited her instead of me. And then—like a burning bush plummeting out of heaven—inspiration struck for the next bit:

"To my little sister—"

Yes! I could address the toast directly to the bride and groom! Oh ho ho, I was made in the shade. The rest would flow like wine from a wine box.

To my memory, the rest of the night is a whirlwind of eraser dust and exhaustion. But before dawn, I had a toast:

> To my little sister: I always knew you could be
> a pain with a capital P. And now you've made it
> official. Congratulations.
>
> And to Mr. Pain: I always wanted a brother. But my
> parents, whom I love anyway, failed to give me one
> in four valiant attempts. I look forward to getting
> to know you better, and finding out what's so great
> about fart wars, really.

And then I said some stuff about love and support, and cultivating your own happiness, blah blah blah, it's not important because I didn't get all emotional while reading it and I totally didn't even cry so what's it to you.

Ultimately, my one Responsibility was a success, because no one even remembers what I said. After all, people remember only the things you muck up at a wedding. And it turned out that I was way ahead of the game with my midnight writing. Mrs. Pain wrote up her vows that morning, when she had nothing else to do besides hair and makeup and cry and redo makeup and keep her dress unwrinkled. Whereas I, unburdened, was free to think about maybe finally shopping for my wedding clothes.

Grammar
Sutra

I HATE TO TELL YOU ALL that I am not yet so wealthy as to receive invitations to spend the rest of my carefree life on Trillionaire Island. This, despite investing my entire child-hood life savings in baseball cards. But lucky you, because I'm still here to talk about sex!

Actually, I'm here to talk about grammar. But by incorporating sex, I got you to keep reading. Numbers can be made to show that reader engagement increases by 152% if a first paragraph suggests free-range body parts and nothing at all about grammar.

The same fact is true for dating, incidentally. You typically should not discuss grammar on any date, from the very first one until death do you part.

Just because you shouldn't discuss grammar on a date doesn't mean you shouldn't use good grammar to seduce your date. Notice I didn't say *correct* grammar. People who use correct grammar are like that kid in elementary school who invokes the infield fly rule during PE kickball: They have no friends. If they had friends, their adult conversations would sound like this:

"I need a shoulder on which to cry."

"Why is that?"

"My sentences sound stilted; as such, no one will sleep with me."

This conversation obeys the grammarian's commandment Thou Shalt Not End Sentences with Prepositions, Nor Other Inappropriate Parts of Speech That Thou Knowest Not. But rules are made to be broken by innovators and heroes. So here's what happens when that rule is broken:

"I need a shoulder to cry on."

"Why's that?"

"My crevasses are chafed. I never realized all the things two or more healthy adults could use fresh produce for!"

This conversation does not use entirely correct grammar. But it uses *good* grammar, which helps you make yourself understood while not standing out as a loser who cares about grammar. Talk good, and you're halfway to getting it on with potential sexytime sidekicks.

For instance, even the simple act of suggesting "Hey, we should get it on!" ends with a preposition, so long as you ignore the exclamation point. I looked up what a preposition is for you; it's a word that describes the relationship between other words. These terms come in handy in the bedroom, or wherever you prefer "getting it on." So, if you want to put something "in" something else, or "through" it, or "under" it, or "between" it, you need a preposition as well as healthy interpersonal skills and a prophylactic of choice.

This good-grammar communication strategy is a critical component of a healthy sexual relationship. Two or more adults must be able to relay their desires, limitations, and curiosities, not to mention addressing sexual acts by their proper slang terms. Use your imagination here and fill in the blanks:____ it off; ____ it out; and so on.

Our own distinct tastes determine what we slide in those blanks, but almost any truly adventurous sex act ends with a preposition. Think, like, "Knock it off!" or "Cut it out!" If one uses *correct* grammar, those sentiments are impossible to convey concisely and accurately in the heat of the moment.

Yet *good* grammar is about more than sex; it is about building a foundation of lifelong bliss by manipulating situations to get what you want. Let's analyze the Prepositional Commandment using a familiar example.

> **EXAMPLE 1:** "Honey, do you need a shoulder to cry on?"
> **QUALITY OF GRAMMAR:** Good.
> **ANALYSIS:** 87% likely to encourage spontaneous shoulder snot-stains now instead of later, when you have plans to watch the Big Game.

> **EXAMPLE 2:** "Go cry somewhere else. You're blocking the TV."
> **QUALITY OF GRAMMAR:** Impeccable; you might even say honest.
> **ANALYSIS:** 100% likely you can watch every Big Game you please for the rest of your life, because there's not much else to do when you live in a full-body cast.

Grammarians and other nuns will have you believe that correct grammar equates to strong morality. Whether you believe them or not, they are wrong. Correct grammar equates to sleeping at your brother's house for a month, until the divorce is final.

Good grammar, on the other hand, is clearly flexible and beneficial. It's only tricky because it changes depending on the context. The phrase "dual carb mod," for instance, probably makes all kinds of sense in a mechanics' shop or a nutritionist's office, but it is not a phrase to use lightly around even reasonably proficient columnists. We earned English degrees precisely so that we could avoid such layman speak, and also crescent wrenches.

Wherever you roam, remember: the key to good grammar is to communicate clearly, by any means necessary. And finishing sentences with prepositions is what good communication is all about. If you disagree, you can just ____ off.

Rhymes
with Rubes

APRIL IS NATIONAL POETRY MONTH, and I am touched to be the one reintroducing this lost art form to the masses. This includes people like you and me! Because odds are, we don't understand poetry.

Poetry has lain dormant since history days, murking up its modern-time meanings. What I can tell you with authority is that poetry used to be a noble calling, largely because humans had not yet invented doctors. Once we could compare it to medical science, we got the notion that poetry was *hard* and did not earn actual money. Plus, with doctors on hand, people weren't all dying by the age of twelve. With all that extra life-expectancy time to challenge our brains, build our vocabularies, and deepen our understanding of human nature, we as a species chose to browse pictures of puppies jumping into swimming pools after tennis balls instead of doing poems.

But poetry does not die easily. There is no other way to explain why I was supposed to read both *The Iliad* AND "The Red Wheelbarrow" in high school. Tragically, modern-day-me was not around to teach high-school-me to better appreciate poetry's efficiency and utility, literature's answer to the *Sports Illustrated* sand bikini.

Though I was too late to save myself, I am now poised to help poetry pounce on a comeback. We live in an age of short media, such as gifs, 140-character journalism, and Seth Green. Why not turn to poetry?

Probably because so much poetry these days is, objectively speaking, bad. That's what happens when a society tries to prioritize science, mathematics, and human rights violations over true art. Yet the quality of poetry does not negate its publishability! Plenty of presses print volumes of carefully chosen poetry submissions for the super low price of FREE.*

Still, quality work is often buried among such wastelands of drivel. For instance, in the fifth grade, I composed a rousing epic about the RMS *Titanic*—*way* trendier than the lame movie, although unfortunately with less nude portraiture. My poem was chosen for publication by one such press because I was clearly a Wunderkind. My parents were so proud, they snipped $45.00 out of the grocery budget to buy my book.

I pity the other, self-appointed "poets"—all those poor saps suckered into filling out my volume of poetry by purchasing copies for their distant relatives, secretaries, garbage collectors, and spouses. But don't let the publishing houses deter your pursuit of poetry; they will do *anything* just for money. The true poets out there are in the poetry biz for all the right reasons.

The right reasons are simple, given a few qualifiers. Writing a short, meaningful, artistic poem is something all deep and attractive people do in order to become both embarrassingly wealthy and immortal. Plus, it's easy. Want proof? Here is my own edgy and spontaneous composition:

---

*With purchase of five or more copies at the one-time wholesale price of $45.00 each.

Roses aren't red.
The sky isn't blue.
The distinctions between colors are a subjective
     phenomenon adhering to social regulations and
     contextual indicators; colors, in other words, are
     not definite, and our perception of them relies
     on linguistics, cultural norms, and possibly our
     own personal color wheels.
This poem is so edgy, it doesn't even rhyme.

Eat your heart out, T. S. Eliot. And speaking of crowd-pleasers who craft non-controversial hits on the fly, even you can be goaded into creating poetry, so long as you too are deep and attractive. Absolutely any poet can trick graduate students into mistaking their poetry as "metaphoric" or "possessing meaning" by using only the sex-advice section of the newspaper, or a page anonymously donated from your sister's diary.

Here's how. Go through the paper, circling your favorite words, either for sound, definition, the shape of the letters, or all of the above (as in the case of the word "boobs"). Then circle other words to link those words together, and bam! you have a poem.

Below is an exemplary example of the "found poetry" technique, using words from this selfsame chapter to hone a Meisterwerk of a poem that is equal to the sum of its parts:

Noble sand bikini
Poised to prioritize quality.
Super low, a rousing,
Snipped, deep and attractive
Crowd–pleasers
Using only boobs.

This technique, unlike other so-called "arts" that require chunks of marble or alpaca-hair brushes or training, is actually feasible. Seriously, even a pet parakeet can make this kind of poetry in the bottom of its cage. And who can judge the quality of little Fluffmugget's creative genius?

I can. And I'll consider it for publication, if you enclose just $45.00.

Ursinine
Behavior

EVER SINCE I GREW UP watching Kermit the Frog reporting for *Sesame Street News*, I have plowed into the field of journalism with a singular goal. I crafted my education, careened up several career ladders, and enhanced my résumé with the sole driving motivation of holding a baby bear cub.

You may see the flaw in my dream: baby bear cubs, after all, come from adult mama bears, who are much less domestic and docile than the one whose house Goldilocks burgles. I long ago gave up on my goal, because I had not bothered to find a way around this maternal deterrent. I finally accepted that my dream was some cruel mirage, the lone unattainable fantasy from my dorm room days.

But then I brushed so close to my dream that I could smell it. Which is, admittedly, not very close. A bear's scent shades more acreage than a solar eclipse. If you could hear a bear's odor—and I'm not saying you can't—it would sound like busted speakers playing Tom Waits on a dubbed cassette tape through the PA system in the Astrodome, which, remember, has been partially demolished.

Still, this was close enough to discover that holding a black bear cub is a real, honest possibility for a journalist with friends with sedatives. Mere weeks ago, a newspaper that runs my column featured a piece about precisely that.

The journalist who covered this story shall remain nameless because I'm not speaking with her ever again until she shares more pictures. And boy, are there pictures. One reveals the journalist cuddling the cub inside her jacket. With shots like that, she will never have to change her profile picture ever again.

This journalist may be lucky, but her luck's not dumb. She enlisted a team of scientists to tranquilize the mother bear. To justify their grant money, the scientists busied themselves pretending to weigh the bear, count its teeth, and glance nervously at their watches, only this last one was not pretend.

The botheration is, I was available at the very moment someone decided to go into the wild, sedate a bear, and squeeze its cubs. I don't have any idea what I was doing at that moment; but, to fulfill my lifelong aspiration, I would drop practically anything so long as it wasn't another lifelong aspiration. And those don't come along but once a week.

Yet I did not receive the editorial rose for this assignment. Never mind that I have survived all my past encounters with wild bears—once would be luck; twice must be talent. And speaking of talent, I have four little sisters and never once changed a diaper. Isn't that precisely the wherewithal you want on a cub-hugging expedition?

At first I was wounded deeper than any startled bear could gash me. But I gradually realized that I'm not that kind of writer—which is to say, one motivated by such unimportantries as "deadlines" and "facts." Also, I am re-evaluating my dreams.

Judging by nameless Tracy's photographs, bear cubs are the size of air-cooled Volkswagen engines. One of those has got to leak more than the other; I don't want *my* clothes finding out which. And I can totally hold that much weight without grunting, but I have too much respect for wildlife.

Like, this one time in college, we heard a screeching from underneath the porch. My neighbor and I armed ourselves with police surplus floodlights to locate the source: an abandoned, terrified, and ferocious baby cat. Protected by thick leather gloves and an awesome respect for this feral creature's fear and claws, we waited until the modern-day Crocodile Hunter who lived next door came home and rescued us.

The way I see it, there are only two reasons for exposing your flesh to a wild animal: 1) You are a trained professional; 2) The situation presents an Educational Opportunity, wherein you learn not to expose your flesh to wild animals.

Or there's the Canadian way. Parks Canada researchers are mounting extreme-action-capturing GoPro cameras on locomotives. To guarantee *their* grant money, these research-ers decided to study how grizzly bears react to oncoming trains. The premise of the study is that *everyone* reacts to on-coming trains. You can't not wave, or twerk your head like you're watching a one-way tennis match, or time your imagi-nary self dashing across the tracks at the last moment.

But apparently, the grizzlies don't react appropriately. The researchers hope to develop Educational Opportunities so they (the bears, not the researchers) stop getting in the way of friggin' trains already.

Their scientific method is indubitably awesome. How-ever, these researchers have missed the primary point of photographing wildlife, which is human safety.

For instance, the nameless paper that runs my column's photographs saved me from my own ignorant desire to cradle-rob a mama bear's den. The journalists courageously hugging cubs out there are raising all kinds of such awareness, including something about feeding the bears, something something, it's a good idea to leave garbage on the front porch.

Check out my rockin' reportage! I ought to earn my trench coat and microphone any day now.

Om Mani
Pedal Huh?

I've GROWN TO LOVE EVERY BIT of tradition surrounding Pops' and my participation in the annual Iron Horse Bicycle Classic: the pre-ride pasta dinners, fretting over the weather forecast, griping about how the finisher T-shirts aren't as good as they used to be.

The actual butt-in-saddle time has become stagnant, though. It's as if completing a repetitious movement over and over for fifty straight miles is an ingenious idea for a special sub-circle of Hell called Monotony. (Not to be confused with the much brimstonier circle called Monopoly.)

I sorely needed a way to spice up my training this season. And I had no shortage of ideas. Too bad most of them stunk. Steroids? Too expensive. Unicycle? I lack the appropriate handlebar mustache. Fresh new training routes? Nah. I don't like change.

Then it hit me. An idea so radical, so counterintuitive, it could run for President. If some percentage of cycling is mental, then I could train my mind. And if I could do anything I put my mind to, then I could train for the Iron Horse *without even riding a bicycle.*

So that's how I did it.

Now I'm not saying I sat around all lazy this spring, deluding myself into thinking I could climb mountains without practicing. Rather, I meditated.

If you're like I was four months ago, you may think you know what meditation is. But it ain't all humming and sitars. And it ain't all you-can-walk-on-coals-because-you-feel-no-pain either, which put a real damper on my post-Iron Horse party plans. I found out what meditation was really like when I signed up for an intro class at the local Dharma center.

From the get-go, the class made it clear that this was no get-enlightened-quick scheme. We beginners were dedicating six whole weeks to our burgeoning practice. At one class a week, ninety minutes a class, that's more man hours than I gave to graduate school. Plus, this time, I had to do homework.

Oh yes, homework. We learned all about basic meditation in the first class, and our homework was to practice at home for five minutes a day. Five minutes of being present with our bodies and our breathing. Five minutes of accepting ourselves. Five minutes of being in the moment, not in the past or future, neither here nor there, not anywhere but wherever we had seated our butts.

But—and I cannot stress this enough—five minutes is shorter than any productive bike ride. So I gave myself over to the practice. I cleared my mind of questions and judgments. Breathe in ... breathe out ... breathe in ... breathing feels nice ... I should really breathe like this more often ... like in the checkout line at the grocery store ... that would be zen as fuck ... milk—I should get milk; I think mine expires soon ... or did it already go bad? Man, I suck. I can't even feed myself like a basic human being. Oh, that reminds me, I need to—

DONGGGgggg goes the singing bowl app on my phone, and five minutes are *poof,* and I take one last deep breath after the timer, the meditative equivalent of flossing to fool the dentist.

It is incredibly challenging to sit for five minutes without thinking about things other than your present experience. In fact, pretty much any thought you can think of is shinier than just sitting there. But if one is planning on riding the Iron Horse, one must realize that the Iron Horse takes one considerably longer than five minutes. The ability to exist in the moment, without a hankering for all the beer one is going to drink after one survives, is a handy skill to hone.

I wrestled with meditation for weeks. Like many great heroes of the collective human consciousness—Hercules tackling the minotaur, Beowulf tussling with Grendel, Mario bouncing on Bowser—I strove to bend meditation to my will and make it bring me superpowers. Five minutes, ten, twenty at a stretch. Yet all it brought me was laundry lists of other things I could be doing.

I gave up. And that, dear readers, is when it worked.

The meditation practitioners have nice ways of saying it. "Let go," they say. "Be with your practice." They use words like "invite" and "welcome" and "accept" and "allow." Really, all they are saying is "Throw in the towel! Quit trying, and you might actually get somewhere."

That meditation was one of the transcendent experiences of my life. I now understand getting ahead by giving up. So keep your eyes open for me on the road—I'll be the rider in nirvana. Stop and say hi! And then ... maybe give me a lift?

Pees and Queues

I RECEIVED SOME KICKBACK over disparaging comments I made about Hotmail a while back. Hotmail is technically an email provider that was all the rage for about four days in 1997. It is the communication service favored today not only by young Russian singles looking for to marry a kindly Amerikan gentlemen but also by, it turns out, one of my publishers.

I believe my exact words were—and I'm paraphrasing—that Hotmail is a quaint anachronism that deserves special consideration when it is finally tossed into a dumpster fire and destroyed forever.

Here, then, is my formal heartfelt press-release apology to all you fine young Slavic bachelorettes and Mr. Aragon: I was wrong. I should have singled out AOL instead.

AOL, formerly America Online, first slid into our homes and hearts when it offered families a popular bundle with internet, email, news, instant messenger, and screeching modem.

Before AOL, technology was mysterious and inaccessible, like an Aztec god or the missing remote control. AOL revolutionized that archaic approach to technology. To gain customers, it sent every member of your household a start-up CD about thirteen times a week. This taught my sisters and me that technology was cheap and disposable, and that CDs make really great air-hockey pucks when you fling them over linoleum surfaces. (I'm not saying we personally played a part in the demise of tangible music albums; I'm just saying that you cannot get good velocity from an mp3 file.)

If I had reason to think about AOL, I would presume that modernity had left it munching dust in the taillights. After all, we today have quieter and more portable technologies, like smartphones and the Etch-A-Sketch.

How very wrong I would be! AOL, it turns out, has the most successful business model of the human era so far. More than two million Americans—or the approximate total of registered voters—still pay more than twenty dollars a month in actual money for AOL's dial-up internet service, even though no one uses it.

The strategy is brilliant. AOL gets money for nothing. And the consumer probably sees upsides, too! For instance, when you finally call to cancel your AOL subscription, you will not have to wait on hold to speak to AOL's last remaining call center representative.

This perk cannot be underestimated. Waiting on hold is *the worst*. It's like standing in line at the bank, only I don't get a free pen for my troubles, the kind with the little chain attached.

Also, being on hold completely restricts my freedom. Here I am, at home, comfortably wearing my pajamas (if anything), and yet I feel immobilized. The recorded lady voice always assures me that a representative will be with me "shortly." "Shortly" covers all manner of sins, yet I can't shake the feeling that, just this once, "shortly" might actually mean "soon."

"Shortly" means I can't take a bite out of this block of cheese, because as soon as I fill my mouth, a representative will answer and I won't be able to communicate how he may help me. "Shortly" means I can't take a power sander to my skull in order to dull the sensation of tinny and repetitive classical music, because then I won't notice when I get accidentally disconnected with no way of regaining my spot in line. "Shortly" means too bad about that last cup of coffee; I have to hold it.

I called my health insurance provider three times in the past month about enrolling before the deadline. I sat on hold for more than ninety minutes each time. When I wound up on hold a fourth time, I said *screw this; I ain't holding it no more.* I carried the phone into my, ahem, private office. What were the odds of an actual human answering the phone in the next twenty minutes, anyway?

The conversation went like this:

INSURANCE REPRESENTATIVE: "Hi, my name is Dennis. May I get your name?"
ME: "Please hold for a moment."
DENNIS *[flustered]*: "I'm sorry?"
ME: "It'll be quick."
DENNIS: "Sir, I need to verify your account to pull up your file."
ME: "And I need to verify that I'm clear to pull up my trousers."

In the end, Dennis and I got along great; he instructed me to try enrolling online again, and to call back if I did not succeed. Dennis is smarter than he sounds—he knows I will never call back.

As your most trusted news personality, I will never stick you in such a helpless situation. That's why, if you are in the least unsatisfied with the lowbrow turn of factual events in this piece, you may send your complaints directly to my quality assurance team email (most certainly usually staffed by an actual human being) at *Customer ServiceAOL@hotmail.com.*

They respond to every letter shortly, guaranteed.

Nap and Gown

CONGRATULATIONS, GRADUATES OF THE CLASS of the current calendar year. This is a time of celebration, for it is the first time in living memory when no one in my immediate family is graduating from anything.

But you are! And that's great! I'm certain your families, out there in the audience, don't mind pretending to be happy sitting through all these speeches by strangers with vague and questionable relevance to your class. Instead of spending their day watching all the *Godfather* movies in a row, your loved ones are enduring this multi-hour ceremony just so they can hear your name mispronounced for an approximate total of 1.1 seconds.

Do not underestimate the dedication this takes. With you graduates all dressed the same, your families cannot even bide their time by commenting on your classmates' poor taste in leggings, which really should seldom ever be worn as pants. Seriously. If you learned nothing else in this specific program or course of study, please, please recognize that you would be better off wearing chain mail made from beached kelp than leggings as pants. That look is nearly as unfortunate as jeans worn so low that they are technically denim socks, as the youth did in my day. Either this latter fashion blunder has blissfully gone out of style, or else I have just stopped leaving the house.

Leaving the house. That is what you graduates are doing, in the metaphorical sense. And maybe even the literal sense, if this isn't a kindergarten graduation. A word of advice as you step into the big wide world:

Actually, never mind. I was going to intone something Deep and Meaningful, something using a preschool-sized finger-paint handprint as an extended metaphor for how you will always continue to grow and learn, even though you're leaving school precisely so you can stop growing and learning. It was going to sing such phrases as Next Chapter and Be True to Yourself. It was inspired.

But I have sat through plenty of speeches given by folks who thought they were inspired. And all I remember about them is how bored I was. No one wants to be here; luckily, the person who invented graduation ceremonies also invented alphabetical order. That way, the Aarons get to skip out early, and entire Youkilis families can take a nap until at least the Willises. Or they would, if they could. But they can't.

I realize you graduates take naps for granted. Someday, as adults, you will have to attend graduation ceremonies in which you are not personally graduating. Then you will learn that the folding chairs and bleacher benches in these places are *really* uncomfortable. Unlike you, who have had lots of recent practice napping through social studies class, your families cannot fall asleep on a tile floor or a writing desk or an anthill. They are out of napping shape.

Graduates, you must treat your naps with the rigor and respect of an Olympian. The swimming and running kind, not the curling kind. The ability to fall asleep anywhere, at any time, and to wake up reliably before dinner requires more dedication than you could ever imagine. Once you fall out of practice, once you dull your abilities, once you succumb to the pressures of the waking world ... it's lights-out for naptime.

Or should it be lights-on for naptime? I don't know—and that question has kept me wide awake for hours, entire minutes even, that I would have rather spent napping. But I got lazy with my naps. Scientists say I could have developed higher alertness, enhanced memory, improved performance, less stress, and other superpowers just by crashing out. Instead, I am nap-flabby. Take a long, hard look at me, graduates. I am what happens when you adopt a lax training regimen.

So when you leave here today, by all means, celebrate. Go to dinner with your families, and then party with your friends. Sign yearbooks, hug each other, and swear you are going to stay in touch, even though, in reality, you will get really good at passing each other in the grocery store while pretending to examine the nutrition labels on boxed mac & cheese. Exhaust yourself, so that when you get started on your future, it begins with some killer zees.

You'll keep taking those naps if you want to really Be True to Yourself in the Next Chapters of your life. Let nothing stand between you, your pillow, and a healthy lifestyle. Got a commute? Squeeze one in during the bumper-to-bumper. Got religion? Snooze through the eyes-closed parts of the service. Got ambitions? Don't chase them down half-dozed. Got family? Make sure that they never, ever graduate from anything, ever.

A Man's House
Is His Hassle

THERE COMES A TIME IN A YOUNG MAN'S LIFE when he must make a decision about just how important to him a special someone is. Does he take the plunge and commit to a lifetime of shared joys and sorrows, coupled with joint engagement in the great financial system of the United States of America? Is now the right time to commit, or will better opportunities come along down the road? How will they handle it, this young man might wonder, if, for example, they disagree on the color scheme for a new suite of kitchen appliances?

The young man in question may wish he'd never even heard the biggest question ever to be popped in a committed relationship: "Hey, wanna sell my house?"

The story is old as time, but since you insist, here's the dossier: the Darling Fiancée bought this house in her pre-me life. Then the market sank like a brick with another brick tied to its leg. She and I got together and skipped town.

But it turns out houses aren't like children: they don't go away when you abandon them. So, like cats stalking a crippled cricket, we've waited patiently for the moment when the cricket is no longer upside-down and we can try to sell it to some other suckers.

That moment has arrived. Yet the buyers are not flocking. I finally understand the old James Dean motto: "Dream as if you'll live forever, because that's how long you'll be stuck with your mortgage."

Needless to say, these last few months have been so very trying for a patient, sympathetic, understanding fellow such as myself. I'm sure these are tough times for the Darling Fiancée too, but she is at least acquiring something called "equity" while I receive nothing in return for my struggles.

Here is my secret to handling such hardships with grace, which I read about in an actual printed book so it might be legitimate: Feeling grateful lowers stress and increases joy. So let me tell you about how grateful I am to be selling a house that's not even mine!

I am grateful for handymen who don't show up when they promise to. Not only do I get to dedicate entire weekends to tightening sink faucets—in their magnanimous flakiness, these handymen routinely save us enough money to buy pizza and beer for ourselves.

And let's give a shout-out to real estate professionals everywhere, who are truly not at all to the housing market what pimps are to the horizontal entertainment industry. Despite what people say, real estate agents are genuine humans with families and emotions of their own. I'm grateful for one agent in particular—let's call him "Dick" because that is his name. Dick has taught me all the Sven and Ollie jokes I need to end an otherwise rollicking social gathering. But real estate agents are good for more than that. So I hear. For instance, when it comes to actually selling a house, there's no one better to add all the whimsical apostrophes' to your brochure's.

I think our best hope of unloading this house is a natural and/or manmade disaster that the insurance company cannot write off as an Act of God. Actually, that's where we're in luck. Potential housing disasters happen now more than ever.

I'm not talking about sinkholes in Florida swallowing houses whole. I'm talking wholesale suburban destruction. The *New York Times* ran a piece about shifting soils destroying foundations across this great nation, probably due most likely to climate change, possibly, if it exists. Too dry? Too wet? One then the other? Hello, cracks in the walls!

But, frankly, we need more than compromised structural integrity to get rid of this house. We need Sharknado-style dismantling of the property. Which is why I am now a firm supporter of the fracking industry.

States such as Oklahoma and Texas, which have widespread fracking, are seeing massive spikes in earthquake activity. Oh, sure, some officials claim that "there's no definitive causal link between injection wells and the ground going wobbly," but my belief in the connection is stronger than any scientific "fact."

I would be grateful for any large fracking corporation who wants to operate on the park just up the road from this house. It's a win-win situation: the corporation makes an insane amount of money, and the ensuing earthquakes—Acts of Man and Not God if ever I saw one—take this house off our hands.

If that doesn't work, at least the fracking company will bring in workers, who will need housing. We'll let the Realtor's work out the detail's.

A Man's Kneads

THE BASIC IDEA OF A MASSAGE is to soothe and relax your body and mind, which you accomplish by going into a dim and unfamiliar room, taking off all your clothes, and lying down with your eyes closed. Only then do you allow a stranger to enter the room and touch you in thirty-minute increments.

Taking my clothes off is not an issue. *Au contraire*. Used to be, legend has it, you couldn't keep me dressed. As soon as I got home from play dates or the grocery store—BAM! Pants off. Running around, happy as a billy goat in a tin can factory.

I was like that even as a little kid.

No, the real issue in the whole massage scenario is that this licensed stranger might take advantage of the situation and attempt to force me, while I am both naked and captive, into horribly awkward conversation.

Going into my first full-body massage, this dread of conversation outweighs my fears—common massage fears, according to the internet—of surprise erections, the massage therapist secretly judging my surprise erections, and actually managing to relax so much that I fart.

With such rampant and realistic horrors awaiting, how could I possibly chit-chat? And when I am cornered into conversation, which is worse: Making up answers to which essential oil I prefer? ("Sandalwood" sounds safe, and perhaps "ochre.") Or stonewalling the person who is lending more intimate attention to my entire body than all but the most involved airport screeners?

All this anxiety over massage etiquette and protocol is stressing me out. If I didn't need a massage before, I sure need one now.

When I arrive for my massage, the therapist—let's call her "Julie," because that is her name—shows me around the room and explains, in general terms, what is what. I don't understand much of what she says because I'm too busy hoping that she changed the sheet on the massage table since the last client and his surprise erections.

Julie then leaves me to get naked. In fairness, she explains that I may get as naked as I am comfortable with, but that undergarments can inhibit the effectiveness of the massage on important muscle groups. (She does not mention *which* important muscle groups.)

While she's gone, I poke around like a dog in a strange new room about to get a massage for the first time. I must admit that the atmosphere is soothing, what with the meditative music, all the framed certificates on the wall, and the fact that I'm not wearing pants.

And I start to wonder, not about Julie, *per se*, but about other, more hypothetical licensed professionals on whom I am not about to confer my physique. Why do we trust pieces of paper on the wall just because they are framed? I mean, they could say literally anything, like

FWAGBOTHAM KLIPNIGGET
SERVIKUT PARFMUHN
01 APRIL 2137

and so long as it is not set in Comic Sans or accentuated with clip art, I will think it's foreign and quite official indeed.

Before Julie busts me staring pantsless at the walls, I climb onto the table and veil my nethers with the provided towel. And I spend several moments finding the least awkward position to nestle my face in the face cradle. It's like a hemorrhoid ring. For faces.

Granted—*granted*—I don't have any ideas on improving the luxury and comfort of the apparatus. But for all the funds politicians want to take from education, at least some of it needs to go into face smusher R&D.

Soon, Julie knocks. The sounds I make through the face smusher must sound like "come in," because she does. And though I am a man of seven or eight hundred words a week, I have very few to describe the massage. All my misgivings melt away like dissent under a benevolent dictator.

Julie converses, sure enough, but unlike the dentist, she doesn't expect essay responses. She uses her powers to educate me about caring for my muscle groups. Rather than mash my knots, she works through their layers. I didn't even know muscles had layers! So not only will I walk out of here more relaxed, if I can walk at all; I will walk out of here more knowledgeable about my own body.

That kind of knowledge is pure freedom, children. Like going pantsless for the brain.

Best Chapter in Baseball

MY FRIEND—LET'S CALL HIM "ANDREW" because he is not to be confused with my other friend Andy—recently underwent a Major Life Event. In a two-paragraph email, he told me about the Major Life Event in one sentence. He devoted the rest of the message to baseball. By the end, he invited me to St. Louis to catch a Cardinals game.

I knew precisely one non-baseball thing about St. Louis before arriving: it has an arch commemorating the starting point of *The Oregon Trail* computer game. Even so, I was fully prepared to hate the city.

It's a matter of loyalty. I root for the baseball team on the other side of Missouri, a team far superior to the Cardinals no matter what the standings have read for the last three or so decades. Furthermore, the Cardinals have the so-called and self-dubbed "Best Fans in Baseball." This BFIB claim puzzles me, because it has not been subjected to the scientific method, which I know all about from the tri-fold poster boards I whipped together in elementary school—that is, when I wasn't shooting more bison on the Apple IIe than I could carry back to the Conestoga wagon.

Empirically speaking, a fanbase cannot bear Best Fans in Baseball status when, every single game, they leave so few empty seats for the other team's fans to fill. And what makes them the best—tolerating one of the most efficient organizations in professional sports? Enduring an unsightly eleven World Series championships?

Beats me. But my gut tells me you need more than the Best Front Office in Baseball and the Best Team in Baseball to be a Best Fan in Baseball.

No wonder I felt the need to trash-talk all forty thousand fans at the Cardinals game that Andrew and I attended. But the BFIBs were way too nice to bash. They didn't even make a single negative remark about the Best Hacker in Baseball, the unidentified Cardinals employee who kindly notified the Houston Astros front office that their passwords were out of date.

Drunk on wonderment, I set out to chronicle the other superlatives St. Louis has to offer.

Retroactively, I started the list with the Best Walk in Baseball. This is the five-minute stroll from Andrew's apartment to the baseball stadium, during which we drank beer without the aid of a brown paper bag. This is, apparently, legal in St. Louis, which means they have the Best Laws in Baseball.

After the game, I was exhausted. So we had more beer. Then Andrew put me up on the Best Couch in Baseball. Despite the oppressive mugginess steaming off the Mississippi River, I had what you might call a pretty good sleep.

For the next two days, I noshed my way through St. Louis. I ate the Best Frozen Custard with Hot Fudge on a Brownie in Baseball, the Best Deep Dish Pizza Once Ordered by the President of the United States in Baseball, some burritos, and the Best Pretzels Made by the Family of the Guy on the Steely Dan Album Cover in Baseball. I also ate—note that this is "the number one barbecue in St. Louis"—the Best Memphis-Style Barbecue in Baseball.

Through this adventure, did Andrew and I engage in tenderhearted analysis of his Major Life Event? Of course not. We didn't need to. We are dudes, and we were duding pretty dudely things, like a cigar and whiskey bar. The Best Cigar Tender in Baseball offered us the Best Cigars in Baseball, but we did not have enough connoisseurship in our wallets to appreciate them. So we kicked back in leather chairs, puffed the Best Cigars Our Remaining Budget Could Buy in Baseball, and further outduded ourselves by chatting up (in a dudely way) the Best Totally Not Addicted Basketball Gambler in Baseball.

I asked the BTNABGIB why, in this town, he was not wagering on baseball. Especially considering that the home record of the Cards at the time was, judging by the enthusiasm of the BFIB, approximately 40-2. He perked up at that tidbit and texted someone right away. I'm pretty sure he reinvested his basketball winnings on the surest game in town. For all that St. Louis had provided me, it felt good to give back so constructively to another person's life.

Besides Andrew's, I mean. Thanks to our gastrointestinal spirit and dudely rehabilitation, his Major Life Event will end up being one of the Best Things to Happen to Him in Baseball. And St. Louis turned out to be a pretty rad place after all.

Except for the Cardinals. They stink.

Rerouted

THIS IS NOT THE PIECE I originally wrote. Turns out, I cannot in good faith publish that piece. I will tell you why. But first, I want to show you what I set out to say. It was about modern air travel experiences. You see, I recently flew the friendly turbulence, where a traveler can kick back, sip a complimentary third of a can of ginger ale, and hyperventilate in fear that the plane will make an emergency landing in some place like the Atlantic Ocean or Boise.

In fairness, there is no good reason for me to hyperventilate. I have absolutely zero control over the in-flight movie and other causes of emergency landings. And it's not just me who is futile. Every single human effort to prevent airline-related fatalities has failed. Metal detectors, personal body scans, X-ray machines, sniffer dogs, randomized luggage searches, interrogation rooms, airport Chili's restaurants, and pilot training: not one of them can keep that kid from kicking your seat so hard that the engine falls off.

But we rely on these techniques anyway. These are the prices of traveling across time zones more quickly than you can by hitchhiking, not counting layovers and flight delays.

Speaking of flight delays, I wanted at first to write about how delays seem to be growing more common. I even did research, with actual numbers and stuff. We liberal arts majors agree that the spirit of statistics is more important than the jiggery-pokery "values" of actual numbers. So here are some of the spirited statistics I picked up in a peer-reviewed conversation:

- In 1955, the average expected flight time from Los Angeles to New York was 3.5 hours, and 40% of flights arrived on time.
- By 1985, the average flight time was 5.5 hours, and 60% of flights were on time.
- In the modern era, the flight will be canceled 98% of the time due to weather, corporate merger, or non-applicable use of frequent flier miles.

By now, planes should be going faster *and* landing at their intended destinations. Then again, for all the things that technology was supposed to improve in our lives, I am still waiting for a futuristic device that does _____.

Do you see that blank space? I had to cancel funding for that piece of commentary because I lost the moral right to write my original column. Which is too bad. The whole thing was going to be a doozy. It was going to permanently and irrevocably get rid of waiting in line.

You know the drill. You're standing inside the velvet rope snake, waiting your turn to tell the counter agent that, yes, you packed your own luggage, even though your mother actually did it for you but she's not a terrorist so it's okay. Other passengers are nudging their elephantine luggage into your personal bubble as if they will spur you to advance more quickly. And you're thinking that there must be a better way to spend your life.

It turns out that you are right. Danish researchers showed that the usual first-come, first-served method of waiting in line is the pits. We'd be better off acting like the children in *Lord of the Flies* or the Republican presidential field in any given election cycle. But since I am not publishing that call to action, the airports will continue issuing passengers numb shells of oblivion and Cinnabon, so that by the time we board the flight, we will not notice that we do not, technically, fit inside the aircraft.

I had also written an open memo to my fellow airline passengers regarding seat assignments. Since I cannot now print the memo in full, I hope the memo subject line will suffice:

> SUBJECT: Dear fellow airline passengers: If you take an aisle seat or a center seat on an aircraft, and the window seat with my name on it is not yet occupied, do not proceed to buckle your seat belt, unpack your luggage, and spread your Cinnabon onto three separate tray tables, because you will have to move when I arrive, and I do not appreciate your theatrical sighs.

So anyway, that's what all I was going to write about in this piece. But during my recent travels, my rants were proven fallacious on nearly every count. All four aircraft took off on their scheduled departure date. The lines moved as freely as if they had eaten Raisin Bran. And I avoided Boise entirely. Therefore, as an integrous journalist, I scrapped the scathing original draft in its entirety, in hopes of speeding the return of my misplaced luggage.

Paws Button

A WHILE BACK, I PROMISED to tell you the story about the dog who was afraid of flies. This golden retriever mix—let's call her "Sugar," because that is her human name—exemplifies how people are wonkier than Willy's chocolate factory when it comes to training their pets. This story will butcher you; I myself narrowly evaded death, but it has a happy ending with, as you might recall, Kevin Spacey. **[Editor's note: We still could not afford to reshoot Mr. Spacey's role in this sequel. Please accept our apologies.]**

Speaking of Mr. Spacey, Sugar springs more leaks than the prematurely released third season of *House of Cards*. Leaking is Sugar's primary mode of communication. It's how she indicates hunger, joy, greetings, complex arithmetic, and, most especially, the presence of houseflies.

I first met Sugar when I was going to housesit for her masters. After I hosed off my sneakers, I asked her humans about managing Sugar's self-expression. Their answer was: "We buy paper towels at Costco."

I have housesitted (housesat?) for many people and their many dogs, and I have therefore earned many insights into the nature of animal/human relationships. For instance, did you know that dogs and cats are remarkably intelligent, versatile creatures, capable of adapting to extreme circumstances? Of course you did, because everyone knows that. Everyone, that is, but pet owners leaving town. They write entire care manifestos for their animals, with itineraries and menus more prescribed than the Queen of England's.

Take Caspar the Scottish terrier. His masters believed their dog was incapable of basic canine functions without a treat. Caspar had a "good boy, you woke up this morning!" treat, a "good boy, you came to the kitchen to eat your breakfast!" treat, a "good boy, you ate your breakfast!" treat, and a "good boy, you didn't eat your own doo-doo!" treat. Caspar's humans augured his imminent demise should I vary from this treat-dispensing formula.

Ever the curious scientist, I tested Caspar's mental flexibility. My hypothesis was that, if the trials went sideways, I could just acquire another Scottish terrier, since they all look alike to me anyway.

I cannot confirm the results of my experiments, because they are still being peer reviewed in small claims court. But I *can* suggest that people ought to give me more credit for figuring out their home theater systems.

Entertainment units outshine even the biological, psychological, and metaphysical workings of these people's pets. My clients really hope to make me swoon at all these cables, speakers, readouts, inputs, outputs, controllers, menus, guides, and interfaces. With this here setup—get NASA on the phone, quick—you can play CDs through the same device as your cassette tapes.

I *know*, right?

But I cannot act blasé about the home theater systems, because these people are paying me to be their dogs' friend. So I gasp and whistle when they tell me about how they subscribed to this wonderful new service that sends you movies *in the mail*. You don't even have to drive to the video rental store, which is handy since it's now a Panera Bread. The same company also offers an internet movie service that works right through the TV! The proud owners of this miracle promise to leave their teenage nephew's phone number so he can help me access it.

I've learned a lot by staying in other people's houses. Namely, that when I insist I'll just watch pirated movies on my laptop, I receive the audio/visual tour a second time, only more vehemently.

But I've learned something else, too: that being invited into someone's home is an honor and a privilege. You see, home is the only place my clients can control with no regard to societal standards of dress or aesthetics or odor. Home is the freedom they've yearned for ever since their parents told them they could dump sand on the floor all they want when they have their own house. Home is a sacred space.

So when folks decide to vacate their sacred spaces for weeks at a time, they need someone to entrust with the care of their crotch-licking surrogate children. (Whose crotch? That's up to the fur baby.) They need someone who respects their individual life choices and preserves their unique visions of order. Someone who doesn't gossip about their private lives in a public, printed medium. Someone, in short, who is reliable and keeps every promise—

Crikey! Our time is already up. Next time I write about housesitting, I *swear* I will tell you about how that fly-fearing dog nearly murdered me. It's so epic, I couldn't possibly choose just one detail to tide you over. Meanwhile, if you really need spoilers, you might read the Rorschach blots Sugar left on the floor.

Spin Cycle

WHATEVER YEAR YOU'RE READING THIS, it's been a rough one in the news. People are always saying things like, "Newspapers should run more positive stories, like about that nice young boy who picks up roadside garbage for free." But these people don't realize that no one—not even that parolee doing his time collecting trash—commits truly selfless deeds worthy of print.

No one, that is, except for me. For just as Rumpelstiltskin spun whole roomfulls of worthless straw into precious gold before it broke the camel's back, so I want to puree leftover news into easy-to-swallow gold before anyone else chokes on it.

What follows are ten gristly issues that I have spiced into tastier news morsels. You won't find discussion about these out-of-the-news-cycle topics anywhere else, unless of course you know how to Google.

#10: The Audubon Society, which still relies on artists' renderings of birds rather than just taking pictures on the company smartphone, declares that at least 314 of 588 bird species in North America will be threatened by climate crises this century.

This announcement is a blow to those dedicated citizens who travel the country in hopes of spotting, against all odds, a fellow loon. But to their children, this means liberation! No more must they spend vacations strapped to the back seat like brutalized hostages. By the year 2100, the only places their parents can drag them to observe some stupid birds will be the zoo.

Of course, like the dodo and ~~Lindsay Lohan's~~ Kevin Spacey's career **[Editor's note: Yes, we found the budget to reshoot this joke]**, most of these birds will be dead. Zoos will have to display taxidermied specimens and hope no one notices the difference. Which no one will, because as I discover every time I go to the zoo, any animal not picking its nose (I'm looking at you, cotton candy salesperson) is either asleep or hiding.

Zoos of the future can utilize this phenomenon to ensure their own longevity! Say that there is only one stuffed eagle in all of the United States, not counting whichever president is in office at the time. Zoos could pass around this specimen so that, at any given point, one zoo has a visible eagle. All the others would post a sign that reads, "The bald eagle's stark white head helps camouflage it amongst the green pine trees of its native home—can *you* find it in this chicken-wire enclosure?"

This situation presents a win-win for zoos and patrons alike. The zoos save money on cleaning bird poop off their windows. In turn, they raise admission fees, thereby offering visitors a solid excuse not to buy the cotton candy.

Speaking of American ingenuity …

#9: A Tampa woman undergoes cosmetic surgery to add a third breast, for which she provides actual photographic evidence rather than an artist's rendering. Within a day, several news outlets proclaim the feat a hoax, unless it isn't, but it probably is.

Some railway trains draw power from a high-voltage third rail that runs alongside the tracks. Contact with it is often fatal. The term "third rail" has expanded to indicate any issue so charged as to be off-limits even to politicians.

I vote we change this term to "third breast," because I ain't touching this one.

Speaking of stuffing extra goodies in your shirt and wondering who will notice ...

#8: Major League Baseball decrees that all stadiums must install walkthrough metal detectors or personnel with wands at all entrances.

I will admit, I'm a little worried about this direct move against intentional violence. It could spell the end of the full-contact hot dog races that Abner Doubleday so envisioned as an integral part of drawing hockey fans to baseball games. And you can say bye-bye to the T-shirt cannon, unless the grounds crew invents an equally effective plush model.

Ultimately, though, metal detectors are likely not the worst idea in this list. Professional ballplayers are already not allowed to use metal bats. By cutting down on metal in the stands as well, MLB is purifying the game, which (contrary to rumor) still takes place between the stadium commercials, Wrestlemania-quality player introductions, and trips to the concourse to buy the $12 beers necessary to survive three high-decibel hours at a modern ballpark.

And that's not even the biggest perk! If airport security teaches us anything, it's that metal detectors will protect us from an unanticipated attack of being on time for anything, ever. When the game is about to start, you will still be waiting in line for your Liberty Frisk. This means you will completely miss some early-round-knockout *American Idol* contestant singing, with less irony and more notes than a Vivaldi concerto, about "the Land of the Free, and the Home of the Brave."

Speaking of unfortunate finales ...

#7: A highly anticipated top-ten list runs out of room before coming to an

The Horse
Gets Its Name

ALL THE POWERFUL STORIES OF KNIGHTLY TRIUMPH have those moments when the laurel-sitting heroes pull themselves out of their comfort zones and onto paths of even greater glory. In the case of truly gallant heroes, they also get a horse. My own moment (and my own steed) arrived when I got a mountain bike.

For years now, I have been a road biker exclusively. When people talk about tackling the local trails, I respond with enthused non-committance. "Oh, yeah! Dead Cat Descent. Man. Go you," I say. "Me? Oh, no mountain biking for me right now. I can't risk going all *127 Hours* until I'm done having a functioning, intact skeletal system."

Of course, if I *had* ever mountain biked, I would have rocked it. I just have always had really good reasons for *not* mountain biking, like not having a mountain bike. Then someone had to go and generously give me their old ride.

This bike is no show horse. It is a hardtail, weighs as much as ten road bikes, and—sit down, fainters—sports mere 26-inch tires. I mean, I'm not saying it's the kind of bike you ship to third-world countries along with all the "Super Bowl Champion Carolina Panthers" T-shirts, because at least it has front shocks. All I'm saying is that this bike is a little closer to Ichabod Crane's Gunpowder than it is to Gandalf's Shadowfax.

A rickety steed never stopped a true sportsman, though. So I agreed with myself that I would learn to mountain bike—as soon as I checked the bike out, washed the frame, lubed the chain, adjusted the seat, installed toe clips, pumped up the tires, test-rode it around the block, watched how-to videos online, read the trail maps, consulted my horoscope, and waited for the right weather.

While I waited, I had to come to grips with a certain fact: that excelling at mountain biking meant I would have to excel at falling. Falling was a given. All mountain bikers fall, and then they brag about how many ribs they cracked. To be perfect at mountain biking, I would have to give up on having my face un-smashed by fence posts.

Well, dammit. I could get good at falling. In fact, I made falling a goal. I declared that when I took my steed for its virgin spin, we would ride hard, clear up until the moment I fell.

So this weekend, the stars finally aligned, and my bike could stall me no longer. I rode up to this back training ground at the local college. I went at a time when I expected no other cyclists, so I would have free rein over the grounds. Yet this space is also—in support of the school's interdisciplinary liberal arts approach to all subjects—a frisbee golf course, with several groups of frisbee golfers mingling about.

It would have been easy to let their presence deter me. After all, they might laugh at my poor bike! But I believed in my ride. Screw whatever these frolfers thought of my wheels.

I have to say, parts of my first mountain bike excursion were easy. The easiest parts of all were forgetting that I had brakes, and how to use them. So on the downhills, the bike flailed about like Pokey while I masterfully jockeyed it out of the weeds. But we were doing it—careening through wide, sloping turns. Skidding out on straightaways. Dodging frisbolfers. We even rode over a rock! And to be honest, I don't remember which way we were going when the bike wiped out.

What I *do* remember is getting up, dusting off my Spandex, collecting my water bottle from the brush, and fist-pumping to the sky. I did it! I fell like a pro, and I didn't even fall for ... let's take a look at my phone ... man, my screen sure is shaking a lot ... how does basic subtraction work again? ... nine entire minutes!

Now that may not sound like a lot of time to you pro-level professionals reading this. But to this noob, it felt like—well, like time didn't exist while I was riding. It felt *gooooood*. Like being high on adrenaline and not dying even though you have every right to be dead by now. A lifetime's worth of action packed into nine quick minutes, and it wasn't even prom night.

Although I fulfilled my promise to go until I fell, and even though I suspect I might now require arthroscopic knee surgery, this ride wasn't finished yet. No, no. I still had to make it home, and I wasn't about to let a bunch of frigolfers see me walking my bike back to the road.

Without going into details, we rode back home successfully. I internetted a list of famous horses before the shock wore off and came across Rocinante. Now I've never read *Don Quixote*, but according to the tamper-proof Wikipedia page, "Rocinante is not only Don Quixote's horse, but also his double: like Don Quixote, he is awkward, past his prime, and engaged in a task beyond his capacities."

Sounds like my bike to me.

Tattoo Undo

I AM A PRETTY MANLY DUDE. I mean—not to brag, but—I split a log once. So I'm set. I really don't need to surround myself with heavy machinery and dirty toilets and *eau de ball sweat* to bolster my masculinity.

Because of all my virility, I thrive with very few male compatriots in my life. In fact, I could count my meaningful bromances on one hand, if a hand had six fingers and if dogs counted as friends.

Yet these old friendships have been on my mind as of late—one old friend in particular. Let's call him the Mick to my Keith.

Mick and I tore it up in college. So much of what we did together is unprintable, in large part because no one wants to read about two dudes quoting *Seinfeld* at each other. We also kept running out this joke about getting matching tattoos of a certain well-known mouthy rock-band logo. The inevitable fruition of our humor was always foiled by the fact that we trotted out the joke well after any reputable tattoo parlor was closed for the morning, and/or when we were too spirited on *eau de Shiner Bock* for any such parlor to accept us.

Then, one fateful day, one of us made the joke in the afternoon, when we were as sober as nuns plumb out of communion juice. Real men don't back down from a challenge. And that, dear readers, is how we both ended up with an extra tongue on our bodies.

More than a decade later, another impulse cropped up. Some people get wild hairs to clean the house, or to write a book, or to reproduce the Eiffel Tower with bottlecaps. Me? I got the wild hair to remove this tattoo. I inked it spontaneously. Why not ditch it the same way?

I popped into a consultation at one of the local tattoo removal centers. The tattoo remover woman very professionally and directly explained how she would shoot my skin with lasers to break up the ink in the tattoo. For a tattoo this size, the process should take only about five minutes, she said—five minutes, that is, once a month, for an it-depends number of months.

It's almost like spontaneous decisions made earlier in life can't be hastily erased by money, technology, or the sheer desire to make them go away. Undoing is its own process. And, in certain cases, undoing hurts *so much more* than doing. The removal laser is like a hot thumbtack poked through a taut rubber band, thwak-thwakking your skin four times a second. Just like elementary school all over again! Only more expensive.

It's a rough process. Upon being lasered each month, the tattoo's black outlines blister up like a velvet coloring poster depicting Dante's oeuvre. I keep the site wrapped for about a week and moisturized for four, until I go in again to dissolve the picture a little further.

At first, I was shocked how many sessions this process might take. Now, I'm stunned to watch the tattoo dissolve bit by bit each month.

I assume Mick still has his tattoo. He—or the "he" I knew—was more the type to laugh over spilled blood than to avoid cuts in the first place. But the last time I talked with Mick was the day after his first kid was born, several years ago. Last week, one of those "Your friend of a friend's friend liked this photo of their friend's friend" moments showed me that Mick and his wife now have a second child, complete with matching knit sweaters and a professional photographer.

As far as I can tell, we live all of three hours apart. But when we lived two continents apart during study abroad terms, we mailed each other Dr. Pepper and Shiner Bock and other contraband that required less than honesty with the great United States Postal Service. Now I don't even know his exact city of residence. I couldn't mail him a regular ol' postal-service-regulation-abiding Christmas card if I wanted to.

At least, not through the regular ol' USPS. Let's lick this part of the book and mail it through the ether.

So, hey, Mick. Not everything persists as long as the Glimmer Twins. Even so, our friendship is part of who I am. That's what distinguishes "friendships" from "acquaintances." But the tattoo is not a part of me. It never has been. It's always been someone else's logo slapped on my skin. A good laugh, a conversation starter, and in the end, an emblem for so much that I am now finally ready to shed.

Real men can say they miss another man. I missed you, Mick. But I don't anymore. Instead, I'm just glad we had the friendship we did, when we did. It will help me be a better man when it finally comes time to tally up another deep and dudely friendship.

And whatever else happens in this life, don't worry about me. I've got voluntarily-being-shot-by-lasers to keep my man-cred going strong.

A Leg Up

"TAKE CARE OF YOUR KNEES," older people are always saying to me when I jump off tailgates. "When you're old, you'll realize that you could have gone to the Olympics!"

I always blew off their dire warnings. But now, they have come true: I am not representing the United States of America at the upcoming Olympics, largely because of that crash when I first rode Rocinante the mountain bike.

My wipeout was a pretty big deal. It even made the newspaper, in no small part because I wrote about it for the newspaper. Sure, I could laugh about it at the time. You probably laughed too. I can't fault you. Falling is funny! But joint health is no laughing matter.

My knee hurt after the crash. Fair enough. And then it still hurt the next day. It hurt and it hurt and it kept right on hurting. For weeks, I thought, "I'm as young as ever! It will heal!" Then I crouched to pull a weed, and I basically died.

So I did a thing that no self-respecting American man of the male gender ever wants to do: I took an ibuprofen. And then I called a physical therapist.

I would like to tell you all about my physical therapist, but she must remain entirely unidentifiable, because she controls the current on the electrocution machine. She uses this device at the end of every session; she pastes these electrodes around my knee, turns up the power until I giggle, and leaves me to squirm for untold minutes.

I do have to say, I rather enjoy the sensation of electricity coursing through my leg at sub-Frankensteinian levels. If you have never been strapped to one of these machines, it's essentially like those ab-busting devices you'd slap on your belly to develop ripply muscles while falling asleep eating puffy cheese snacks. And despite electrocuting you, it doesn't hurt, unlike the time I touched the exposed wire on a fritzy hotel lamp.

Speaking of the electrode unit, I recently progressed to a level of current that my physical therapist calls the "Russian stimulation." This term sounds to me like one of many potential acts and/or substances available to tourists in Amsterdam. But she assures me that it is perfectly legal in this country, and that it is not what got all of Russia banned from international athletic competition.

I had never visited a physical therapist before this adventure, mostly because I avoid terms like "rotator cuff" and "disjointed." Plus, I had never really injured myself before. I'm a reasonably fit fella. I mean, not only do I walk through airport terminals instead of using the moving walkways, I also carry all the groceries in one trip if someone else gets the door. That kind of fitness is an irreplaceable component of overall masculine health.

So I was relieved on Physical Therapy: Day One to learn that my knee did not appear to be structurally damaged. I had simply, to use the words I put in my therapist's mouth, bruised the shit out of it. The bad news was that she could do little to mend the bruise.

She also discovered that one of my quad muscles in the injured leg was significantly underperforming, which I think means she's calling it flabby. This sounds like more bad news, but really, it is good news, because she said she could work with muscles more than bruises.

"Great!" I said. "Fix me!"

I showed up to Physical Therapy: Day Two anticipating a spa treatment of ice packs and electrode stimulation. What I got was Richard Simmons without the backup exercisers.

This is the primary problem with health care in America today: you visit a specialist who specializes in a specific way of healing people. Yet *you* have to do all the work. And work it is. It does not matter how many triathlons you try, or how much bench you press; you have not truly exerted yourself until you have taken twenty steps *in a row* off a box.

And that's not all I had to do. Oh, no! I then had to step—twenty whole more times—off the complete *other* side of the box.

I thought for certain I would be fully repaired by this point. But then the assistant scheduled me for two more appointments, during which I would have to step off more boxes. My inability to keep my knee straight while stepping off a box made me want to ignore the whole problem and spend the rest of adulthood avoiding knee-based activities altogether.

But here's what I've learned during the course of my therapy: just because my knee is in pain doesn't mean I am less than a complete being. Taking care of ailing parts of my body is admirable, and it is important. That's not why I keep going back to PT, though. I keep going back for my Russian fix. Enough years of this treatment, and I'll be unstoppable for whichever Olympics comes next! Or I would be, if I weren't already disqualified.

Back to
My Future

I HAVE TAKEN A REAL LIKING to myself. That's why I am thankful for throwing out my back, despite now having to depend on others to tie my shoes.

The pain is really not so horrible; it can't be much worse than a shark bite, or getting run over by a garbage truck. It'll get better. Either that, or it'll kill me.

Just kidding! That's what we back-pain survivors call "sciatic humor," which is intentionally not at all funny because laughing sets our recovery back another two to ten years. Same goes for sneezing, breathing, running a marathon, swallowing a drink of water, and blinking. We basically try not to do anything, ever.

Now please do not think that I am weak, or that I fail to care for my back precisely the way WebMD says I should. Quite the contrary: I am taking the long view of my health. By throwing out my back now, at the ripe young age of it's none of your beeswax, I am investigating the waters of old-person matrimony *before* getting married.

Far too many people litter their first, second, and third wedding vows with the untested phrase "in sickness and in health." At the age most people are when they are young, "sickness" means nothing more than "I drank too many Duck Farts last night." And even after worshipping a trash can at four in the morning, youthful lovers may still want to see each other naked again someday.

But your maladies aren't so sympathetic once your skin starts to shrivel, and your ab goes flabby, and convenience store employees start calling you "sir." People expect the elderly to be infirm. So when you're old and sick, no more chicken soup and Sprite for you! Unless you have a True Love to defend your right to a warm wash cloth and buttered toast, your blood relations will solemnly commit you to your own coffin-sized patch where they can visit you once a month until they forget about you.

And that's just your post as a megastore greeter! You'll stand there for the rest of your life, waving vaguely at anyone who might be a relative—it's tough to tell when they're all backlit by the sunlight outside the entrance, whose doors you won't exit for years at a time—and making everyone feel shame for not taking you home with them.

My point is, no one ever buys the mushy banana.

That's why I'm conducting intensive field research to determine just how much tenderheartedness, patience, compassion, and medication the Darling Fiancée will offer me when I'm old—all while my produce is still relatively fresh.

I've modeled my study after Jane Goodall's famous field work. Which is not to belittle the Darling Fiancée—human women are far more complex in their subtle subtextual communication than your average chimpanzee.

Take, for instance, jeans saleswomen. I have never dealt with one personally, since I strive to buy new clothing about as frequently as Green Party members win national elections. But I have often held the Darling Fiancée's purse while she tours the Wide World of Affordable Fashion. This gives me ample opportunity to observe the subtextual communication tactics of the saleswomen, which boil down to: "*He* can't tell you those jeans are baggy in the crotch, but *I* can, and I'll earn commission to say so."

The Darling Fiancée can slap on ten, fifteen pairs of pants faster than a pit crew changing Dale Earnhardt's pants. This is, incidentally, a big part of why she's marrying me, pending the results of my current field research. Right now, with this back in its current state, I can't even put on pants by myself.

Don't get me wrong; I would gladly live my entire life without pants. But Some People insist on draconian standards whereby a free citizenry, incapacitated or not, must cram itself into trousers before leaving the house, even if the trousers are unlaundered sweat pants.

Not to brag, but our pants-donning teamwork highlights the foundation of our bliss. Working together, we conquer any problem with honest communication and empathy. We are an unstoppable duo!

And then we get in the car.

Since one of us is injured and cannot drive, one of us thinks it is not unreasonable to wince over every crack in the pavement, or to grit one's teeth when the other one of us stops too quickly all the time, or to suggest that those men who hold it to be self-evident that women ought to have their driver's licenses revoked until such time as men no longer exist may not be entirely wrong after all. The Darling Fiancée thinks it's just the sciatic humor talking; I do not correct her, because I cannot currently outrun her.

That she proves so capable of tolerating me under duress gives me faith that she will tackle all of my big health issues with the same sangfroid. Like buying the tissues with the lotion, cleaning the mustard out of my feeding tube, and holding my hand as I take the Last Big Journey.

If my Last Big Journey ends at Walmart, I swear I will greet everyone with the finger.

Motherly Advice

LAST WEEK, I WENT to an Eilen Jewell concert. She sings with a voice as smooth as whipped honey, as smoky as aged whiskey, and as big as boulders, all tumbled together in the finest crystal stemware. I don't know how so much soul fits into a single person so tiny—especially when a baby's already taking up all the extra space.

Between songs, Jewell admitted to having no idea how to raise a child. I thought she was off to a good start by blasting the womb with country-rockabilly-honky-tonk-surfer-waltzes instead of wimpier compositions by hacks like Brahms. Her band nailed every song they played. (Including a certain audience member's request for Loretta Lynn's "Fist City," the classiest ditty about two broads duking it out over a man that you'll ever hear.)

But she opened herself up to maternal advice from anyone with wisdom to share. And that was her downfall.

At the merch table after the show, CD sales floundered because all the marms and grandmarms in the joint built a Wall of Crazy Motherly Opinions that no mere music fan could breach. So even though I could not repay Jewell's outstanding performance with my own parenting advice—namely, *keep singing Loretta Lynn lullabies*—the whole imparting-wisdom thing got me thinking: I'm like Superman. Except writing for the newspaper is my superpower, rather than my coverup.

So I'm through filling white space with selfish ramblings about self-enlightenment and politics and other me-centric topics. It's time to embrace my lifelong passion and talents which I just discovered, and help *you* out for a change.

I give you: MORE maternal advice about parenting! Just what you all wanted.

It bears mentioning that if you want child labor around the house that is both legal and free, you should keep your children alive. This aspect of parenting is easily overlooked, because hey, every adult alive on the planet today survived childhood. So how hard can it be?

Therefore, my first real drizzle of maternal advice is: Don't stress about keeping your kids alive.

Besides, if your children ever teeter too close to perishing, they'll just watch "how to stay alive" videos on YouTube. Kids these days are born with sufficiently heightened levels of tech savvy. In fact, I hear Google is quietly working on cornering the pre-natal consumer market with a new app whose functions and appearance will drastically change the moment I finally figure out how to use it.

Once you stop fussing over trivial issues like "child survival," your energies will be freed up to pursue anything you want. Imagine the possibilities. You could hike the Appalachian Trail, or move to a nudist art colony, or binge all of *Breaking Bad* in a single sitting. Parenting will be the wind beneath your wings.

But—and I mean butt—even the chillest parents must deal with changing diapers. I learned a neat trick during my own youth by having four younger sisters: you can avoid diaper-doody-duty by shrieking and running from the house anytime your tyke fires off a bunker buster.

And when this tactic fails, I simply play pass-the-stink-potato. Pawn the child off to a total sucker. By "sucker," of course, I mean "loving responsible adult." Suckers flock to a baby like locusts to a cornfield. The Eilen Jewell post-concert clearinghouse confirmed this phenomenon. So when you see your cherub scrunch and grunt, offer the bundle of cuteness to the nearest cooing, wide-eyed adult-type person. Then, go hike Everest until the crisis passes or the child turns eighteen, whichever happens last.

The other option for avoiding children's diaper patrol is simply to do away with them. [**Editor's note: Our legal counsel requires us to state that he means doing away with the diapers, not the children.**] The best reason for this method, of course, is that it guarantees mortifying photos to share with your child's future prom dates and senior yearbooks. But besides the enduring hilarity for you and your family, the embarrassment will also callous your child's soft-as-baby-bottom skin. If we raised kids with that kind of shame, nothing else could ever touch them. Our children would be ... *invincible*.

Based on my deep understanding of parenting, raising invincible children is the ultimate goal. Parents battle bullies, disinfect countertops, chew out teachers, and spend hours trying to buckle in these confounded car seats, just to give their kids a chance at living forever.

Turns out, we could skip all those steps by just skipping diapers. All past, present, and future parenting problems: SOLVED. You're welcome.

What's that? You want qualifications to back up all this awesome advice from an expert who doesn't technically have children of his own? Listen, I've got creds way better than "experience." As an outside observer unflustered by the perpetual demands of precocious booger-eaters, I am perfectly poised to offer objective and constructive insights. Think of me like ... like a U.S. Congressperson legislating poverty.

If you take umbrage with any of my advice, remember that at least I turned out normal and balanced. And if you're still not convinced, I have some classic lullabies—for your face.

Don't Try This at Home

WE'VE ALL BEEN THERE. You're washing your dishes for the week, and just when you think you're all done, you flip on the garbage disposal. You don't hear the blades gargling on a cereal spoon. This is a victory in your book. So you turn off the disposal, and you start to walk away, and then you stop because the drain just burped a sudsy gallon of chunky salsa into your sink basin.

I am generally a fan of modern technology. But I am less a fan of ancient technology. Plumbing has been around literally since Roman times. It predates everything else I use in my daily life, with the possible exception of breathing. Yet for all its longevity, plumbing has received fewer updates than my iPhone. And kind of like my iPhone, it works really well, until it doesn't.

So with my sink brimming with Satan's mouthwash, I figured I better take quick action. I dropped everything else I had going on, and I went straight to bed.

Why not? Maybe whatever was stopping the pipes would pass by morning. And I always first attempt to solve home-related problems by ignoring them until they go away.

This method works really well, for instance, with an icy sidewalk. I could risk my own neck to sprinkle salt on the ice. But if I just let Nature run her course, then no human being can give me doorbell panic until at least May.

Plumbing, though, is a more sensitive beast. Because plumbing is entirely concealed by walls and dirt and mystery, you cannot ever actually see what is wrong with it. It simply tells you, in no uncertain terms, that you have a problem, and that problem is you.

Oh yes. Stopped plumbing passes judgments unlike any other house-based issue. Tornado ripped the roof off? That blows. Mice chewed up your insulation and your electrical wiring? Those little buggers. Your plumbing is backed up? WHAT HAVE YOU DONE.

I think we are judged by our plumbing problems because of what we regularly put down the tubes. Each and every one of us does it, except for women, who don't do that. And, sure, you can take a certain pride in stopping the flow of traffic to an entire house. But you at least want to *earn* your bragging rights.

It's the pits when the pipes betray you for something you didn't do. At one point in college, I was visiting my then-girlfriend's parents' house for dinner. I excused myself for a moment, because her father's beer was free but also cheap. I was not there for an inordinate amount of time—it was, in fact, extremely ordinate—and when I pushed the lever, the water did not go down, as is customary in America. (I hear it goes the other way in Australia.)

What does one do in a moment like that? It's not like one can hold back the tide with one's hands. Sure, one can grab every towel in the room and build better dikes than New Orleans has, but when the toilet does not stop gushing, one is left with only minimal choices. Even though one did only a Number One—and it wasn't even a hefty Number One!—one could leave the bathroom and turn right, back to the dining room, back to one's future-ex-girlfriend's parents, and nobly accept the appearance of indisputable guilt despite one's purest innocence. Or one could turn left, through the garage, and deep into the dark, forgiving night.

All this to illustrate that, unlike other life problems, plumbing concerns do not disappear simply because I ignore them. When I woke the morning after my sink yarked the dishwater, I decided I better enter the world of addressing problems head-on.

So I persevered with a slow-draining kitchen sink for another four or six days. And then I opened the cabinet doors under the sink to discover actual pipes. I drew on my intensive training in literary analysis to determine that I had no business under there.

That's when I texted the landlords, because they have a vested interest in maintaining the property and I have a vested interest in recovering my security deposit. They called a real, professional plumber, who came to the house and ran the water for twenty minutes and promptly declared that there was no problem after all.

I didn't believe him until I witnessed the sink drain for myself. It now empties like a champ. That's how I learned this invaluable lesson about home repair, and how it is just like a standardized test: go with your first answer. So next time, I'll just stop doing dishes altogether.

All Work
and No Replay

I DON'T COME OUT SWINGING on the big issues very often. But, hey, if the Supreme Court is allowed to make a big deal out of its declarations, then I'm not keeping silent about instant replay.

In high-level professional sports, a referee (also known as "zebra," "blue," and "are you blind") may use instant replay technology to review a ruling on the field. Sometimes players or coaches indicate their desire to challenge a call by placing dirt, spit, or other foreign objects on the shoes of the referees. Other times, the referees can self-evaluate by going into a booth and watching videos until they confirm that the evidence is inconclusive.

In short, instant replay is a huge problem. I realized this realization this morning. I woke up at bar-closing time to watch the Wimbledon tennis tournament, which, despite the inhumane time difference between Wimbledon and the United States of America, still takes place in England.

I'm no athlete, so I'm allowed to sip on performance-enhancing drugs whenever I please. But I couldn't whip up a cuppa, because the match was already in progress when I rolled out of bed. Sure, I could always brew my coffee during commercial "breaks," but these are engineered to commandeer my focus. Anytime a commercial comes on, I am as rapt as a dog sniffing another dog's puckered furries.

So my coffee was delayed. Just when I resigned myself to gnawing on coffee beans, a player challenged the line umpire's call. This challenge required the chair umpire to confer with the camera robots, which are never wrong. (So far as we know. No one challenges the camera robots.) In my experience with spectating American sports, the review process takes maybe twenty minutes, during which time the commentators determine the correct ruling in thirty seconds and then struggle to fill airtime.

I went to the kitchen and brewed my salvation during the interlude. But when I came back, the match was finished! Turns out, in tennis, instant replay is actually pretty close to instant. Such brevity is the greatest part of the huge problem of instant replay. Fortunately, the entire problem has simple solutions: we audiences need longer instant replays, and we need more of them.

Modern life already places too many demands on us. Official reviews during sporting events should be the guaranteed breaks we so desperately need if we want to exercise, change the oil in the car, brew another coffee, or simply make some quality giggle time with our romantic partners.

By implementing more instant replays, benefits would trickle into other aspects of the daily lives of us sports fans. For instance, the more review time Wimbledon grants me to make breakfast, the more bananas I use. The more bananas I use, the quicker I run out of food in the house, and the more likely it is that I will get to lick Nutella off a spoon for dinner.

But whatever the scrumptious side effects of less-than-instant replays, sports are not about enhancing the pleasure of our daily lives. Sports are about winning and losing. And we can only know who is better when we, as a nation, stop relying on human perception and start employing instant replay on every single incident.

If you still believe in the infallibility of referees, then you have never watched football. A game of football—known by Americans as "real football"—is a mess of approximations. For instance, on a first down in the National Football League, the zebras set the chain markers oh roughly where the ball is. When a football player is tackled beneath seventeen other behemoths, he cheats the ball forward on the playing field. The are-you-blinds never fall for this trick, so they put the ball back to precisely about where it maybe was when the guy got walloped.

Only when the ball appears close to another first down will the referees escort the chain crew onto the field, carefully and attentively, as though the chain crew is bearing Fabergé eggs on teaspoons and not a ten-yard length of chain. The referees then measure the location of the ball down to its final stitch.

Please! If the referees are going to make such a circus of measuring a first down, they should employ a replay crew in Camp David or the International Space Station. Otherwise, they might as well revert to playground rules and declare a landmark for every play: "First down is the brown patch!"

Sure, brawls will break out over which brown patch they meant. Good! Brawls take even longer than replays. A couple of those, and I can polish off a law degree. Just in time to represent all the refs when they lose their jobs.

The Booboo Guru

WELCOME BACK TO THE FOOL'S GOLD Advice Column for Smarties. It's just like *Car Talk*, only more exhaustive. Exhausting? Either way: you can't car-berate me for trying!

The General Public has entrusted me—me!—with righting their lives. I am only too honored to set aside my own priorities for them, because they are proof that I have four actual readers (or at least one reader with four aliases). So I'll crack my knuckles and get right down with my altruistic self.

Scott N. writes to say: "My roach colonies aren't producing enough roaches to meet my demand."

Dear Scott N.: let me first whisk you back to a college philosophy course I took because it didn't have a lab fee. There, I learned about moral relativism. The basic idea of moral relativism is that a person's moral judgment depends on that person's culture, historical time period, and exposure to the album-length version of "Total Eclipse of the Heart." No person's standpoint is inherently superior to another.

This philosophy is incorrect, because there are people in this world breeding cockroaches. Breeding cockroaches is not a boon to humanity. Cockroaches are sufficient cause for various health departments to shut down a restaurant. And I have worked in food service on no fewer than five distinct days; I have seen what all *doesn't* shut down a restaurant.

Furthermore, cockroaches can rend familial bonds. My little sister Kara would do anything for me. But this one time, at our childhood home, she refused to kill a cockroach intent on attacking us. I distracted the invader from atop a barstool, keeping whatever roaches have instead of eyes trained on me, leaving her ample space to smash the aggressor with an anvil or a piano. But she would not do it. I had no choice but to remain on that stool until I graduated high school and could move out of the house. Now that my mother has finally sold the scene of the betrayal, perhaps we can begin to mend our relationship.

You, Scott N., may think you need better roaches to meet your demands. Really, you need better demands.

Speaking of health code violations, we have two separate readers concerned about letting loose in the workplace. Missy M. asks, "Which stall is the best to poop in in a communal work bathroom?" And Andy O. ponders, "What about bathrooms that you can only get to by going through the break room? Poop or not? That door is seeming mighty thin."

You all are so cute, thinking these bathroom predicaments are tricky. Try this on for size: You're working a low-level data-entry job in the municipal government system. You sit on the same government-issue perch day after day, entering data, without sufficient ergonomic training. One otherwise lovely day, you go to do something menial, like opening an envelope, when—*wham!*—your sciatic nerve cinches up in a back-crippling event coincidentally referenced earlier in this book.

Now, your options are few, because your job does not offer you paid leave. You can sit through the rest of your shift and permanently fuse yourself to the government-issue perch. Or you can take your ten-minute break to walk, without actually using any major muscle group, to the nearest underground marijuana dealer, who may or may not recognize you from your exposé on the cannabis industry that got snubbed by the Pulitzer committee. You buy all the pain-relief patches you can afford, because they are lightweight and carrying them back will not tax your back, as well as a gummy because at this point you would try heroin if you thought it might return any mobility to your gait.

You've used up your ten-minute break, so you then enforce your legal right to a bathroom break to apply the patches to your own back, despite the fact that by this point you cannot, in medical terms, move. Your vocal efforts might indicate to bystanders that you are birthing a fully matured Ankylosaurus in there. And you don't even get the relief of a sound BM, even though you must still hobble the gauntlet of eavesdropping coworkers back to your government-issue perch.

Missy M. and Andy O., you Smarties are getting paid to poop. Everyone does it, except women. So own it.

Speaking of disgruntling your coworkers, Donna M. wonders, "Is a Kevlar vest tax deductible if you use it at work to prevent back stabbing?"

Donna M., I certainly hope so! If the sole purpose of a system of taxation is not to give us profound satisfaction from exempting ourselves from it, then I don't want to know why our forebears tantrummed over all that perfectly good tea.

Alternately, I might suggest working from home. You can wear pajamas! Also, people have a much more difficult time stabbing you when they dislike your customer service. So while I hope you all appreciate my helpful answers, I myself am not that worried about being backstabbed. Not even if I got "Total Eclipse of the Heart" stuck in your head.

Registered Offenders

Gifts are cool. Thus, in theory, gift registries should also be cool. I really want to like gift registries in the same way I like the novelty food at minor league ballparks: they combine several distinct things that are independently tremendous. A hot dog in a donut? Cheesecake wrapped in bacon? Buying gifts for people who will someday buy me gifts in return? Yes, please!

But there's a catch to enjoying each of these tandem combinations. Some of the catches are tiny and painless to ignore. For instance, I can easily tune out the negatives while savoring The Peanut Butter and Pepper Jelly Jalapeño Bacon Burger, because I believe calories work differently than the scientific cults claim.

Likewise, giving gifts is a simple deed because I am a generous, selfless individual, no matter what people say. Good thing, too! Gifts are obligatory for every birthday party, graduation party, retirement party, bar/bat mitzvah, Christmas shindig, and casual clambake I attend, and the recipient (or the recipient's designated representative) must always say, "Oh, you *shouldn't* have," even though, if I hadn't, I would get nasty looks while eating cake.

But there is one catch here too great to ignore: even for a generous, selfless individual, gift registries pop gift-giving bubbles like cockroaches pop a ballpark appetite. A wedding registry in particular is an overactive guilty conscience coupled with an anal-retentive Transportation Security Administration agent. A wedding registry says, "You *will* buy the happy couple a gift in exchange for their mail-merged invitation, *EVEN IF* you are not attending for reasons including death, and I will tell you precisely what you are permitted buy them."

This setup also drains the fun out of receiving gifts. Normally, in drafting a wish list, one writes down the things one wants (say, a complete-to-date set of *Star Wars* Lego sets) and any pressing essentials (like an alpaca) and lets responsible adults sort out the surprising details. Not so with a gift registry. A registry forces one to select the brand of alpaca and the precise alpaca features one wants, thereby removing all pretense of amazement and wonder when no one buys it for me.

A not-yet-nuptialed couple must repeat the feature-selection process for all eighteen hundred individual items they think they want. And they must pretend to agree on every single item, because filing for separate his'n'her registries is too reminiscent of a divorce settlement.

If the couple emerges out the other side mostly intact, the finalized registry grants every invited guest a peek into the couple's tastes, which are tacky. (This isn't necessarily the couple's fault. A lot of housewares on the market today look tacky when located in actual houses and not the unrealistically staged showcases at Target, Bass Pro Shops, and Toys "R" Us.)

Furthermore, you can now subject yourself to all the reputable registries online. These online registries are sure to show tech-savvy shoppers and honored guests like you which items have already been purchased, so you feel really schmucky selecting a spaghetti spoon for $6.99 when someone else purchased the 24-piece china cookware set with embroidered fringes and digital readouts for $499.99 (and probably didn't even use a coupon code).

Never mind if you do not know the couple well enough to care how, exactly, one embroiders a china cookware set. Never mind if your love for the couple cannot be measured by a price tag alone, or whether or not you have yet met the bride. The thought is not what counts at weddings. What counts is that the happy couple will permanently associate you with the item you select from the prescribed registry—with zero personalized creative input of your own, mind you—until they donate it to Goodwill.

All I can muster is that a couple must really want to recall my face every time they flip a grilled cheese with their Burnished Steel Substitute KitchenMeister Spatula. Why else would they register for the most unexciting items in the history of housewares, when dozens of alpaca accessories fall in affordable price ranges?

This social navigation is hard work. Perhaps that is the brightest spot of all in the fact that the Darling Ex and I are no longer getting married later this year. Our upcoming Life Event led us each to undertake a great deal of self-reflection about what matters most in our lives. I'm not going to say who was at fault for this change of plans—neither of us is to blame, really, since we're both adults here—except to say through a mouthful of pulled pork parfait that the *Millennium Falcon* is a *totally* worthwhile way for people to show their love.

Rounding Third: An Out–of–Character Interlude

Two outs in the bottom of the ninth inning. Game Seven of the World Series. The opponent's ace throws me a heater. I murder it! The crowd goes bonkers as I win the championship for the Kansas City Royals. After celebrating, I fetch the Wiffle ball from the other side of the house, and I set up to win it all over again.

If each of these imagined championships of my boyhood had earned a real flag, my mom's house would have looked like the United Nations.

I let go of that dream a long time ago. I was not skilled enough to be a world-class baseball player. Or, more honestly, I was unwilling to put in the time to find out whether or not I was good enough. I built fresh dreams atop my fantasy of baseball stardom. Write a world-renowned column. Write great novels. Write anything else I damn well pleased, but write it evocatively and maybe even change the world with it.

Those who really and truly push themselves know how much effort goes into spinning hay into gold. The Royals' erstwhile left fielder, Alex Gordon, was the type of athlete who spun that gold into platinum. He dedicated himself to baseball at a level I wish I would offer to my writing, or to anything, really. Others have penned stories in actual respectable sports sections about the one time he broke his dietary regimen to eat a hamburger. His dedication transformed him from a top-prospect bust to one of the silent stars of a short era in the 2010s.

Back in 2014, he lived my old dream. His Royals were down 3-2 in Game Seven of the World Series. Two out, bottom of the ninth inning. Gordon faced the Giants' best pitcher—a pitcher on the threshold of legend—a pitcher whose name we dare not speak.

That the Royals would play in the playoffs at all, let alone on this stage, boggled the oddsmakers. The Royals were mediocre at best in July of that year. They had no stand-out star. Not even Gordon, whose biggest, most reliable successes were on defense, which fans and analysts both tend to overlook. Then, to lean on a cliché, something clicked. So much of the team stood out in overlooked ways that people started looking.

The Royals turned scrappy and resourceful. They figured out what they do best, and they played that way, even when it went against current baseball conventions.

A bunch of guys having fun suddenly plaused the implausible. They earned the team's first playoff berth in twenty-nine years. They won the Wild Card game after their win probability was literally three percent in the eighth inning. They won seven more straight to reach the World Series.

Forget pigs flying and hell shivering. Anything was possible. I felt it. I mean, just look at me: I was writing a weekly column and had already secured multiple publications—hey, two is a multiple—pleased to run it. Solid accomplishments. More pieces of ether made tangible.

Then, with Alex Gordon at the plate, the whole magical season reached its final out. No one on base, down by one run. The first pitch was a strike.

The most finessed storyteller could not craft a more perfect way to play out this postseason. All the seeming restrictions of life frayed and fell away, turning reality beautiful and glorious and completely ridiculous.

The second pitch, Gordon swatted into center field.

The ball touched the grass. A two-out single. The slimmest deli slice of hope.

The center fielder missed the ball. It skittered to the wall. Gordon sped up for second base.

The left fielder bumbled the ball against the wall, buying a couple seconds more valuable than a lifetime of fandom. Gordon ran for third base.

The left fielder corralled the ball and threw it to the shortstop. The Royals' third base coach read the tea leaves in an instant—Gordon's speed, the shortstop's arm strength, the distance of the looming throw—and he hoisted his hands up into the air. He wanted Gordon to stop.

What do you do? You work hard for years for one goal: maybe a World Series ring, maybe a book. If you're very fortunate, the universe sets up the grand opportunity, or a whole Rube Goldberg of opportunities, just for you. Then, the universe does what it does best. It pulls back its hand, takes a step into the shadows, and lets your own actions determine the finale.

Comedies and tragedies are the exact same stories until this final beat. Everyone ends up in love, or everyone ends up dead. You live forever, or you disappear. In these big moments, you get one or the other. There is no compromise.

Alex Gordon listened. He stopped at third base.

The next batter popped out in foul territory. Game over.

The third base coach made a rational call, and Gordon very defensibly trusted him. He put hope on a respirator for one more batter. He put his faith in his teammate to hit another baseball even though, win or lose, his dash would have been pantheonized.

Probably nine times out of ten, he's out.

But one time out of ten, he lives forever.

Listening to the base coach is the smart choice, every time. I survive by listening to the conventional wisdom of my own inner base coaches. *Play it safe. Don't throw away your chances. Never make the final out on the basepaths.*

Game Sevens are not conventional. Big moments are never safe.

When an entire lifetime of striving is on the line, hope has no value. The universe will not hand you victory. You go for it, or you sit on your heels.

For all my emotional investment, for all I didn't sleep that night, I was zero percent pissed that Gordon did not run home. Time and patience softened this blow when those improbable Royals won it all a year later. But even before 2015 retconned the tragedy of 2014, I played out a fabricated memory of his running home, over and over and over. I still do. Even when he's out by a mile, I am proud of him, this person I will never even know.

That year's Royals team showed me the value of fun, and amazement, and wonder, and dedication, and a fair bit of bravado. The season is long over, the band is broken up, and yet they continue to inspire me.

Here I am, rounding second once again. I'm always and perpetually rounding second. But when I get to third this time, I'm blasting past the base coach. I may get thrown out by twenty-five feet and silence the stadium. Analysts may pick apart my boneheaded decision. But I don't care. I'm through living for hope. The dash for home is the play I want on my highlight reel.

Safe or out, there's always next year.

Reptile
Dysfunction

WHAT DID YOU HAVE FOR BREAKFAST this morning? Who cares! It was not more amazing than what I ate. Not even if you had nachos and beer, which could arguably be the most nutritious breakfast since leftover pizza. I win, because I ate real, genuine dinosaur eggs.

I'm not bragging. *You* have eaten dinosaur eggs, too! Come to that, unless you were born vegan and have remained steadfast, you have probably chowed down on an actual dinosaur.

These claims are not fabrications made up by me in my boyhood when I breathed, drank, and—without knowing it—ate dinosaurs. This is the real world, people. Dinosaurs are not extinct. They live among us, only most of us call them "birds."

"Ha ha, you coot," I can hear you say. "You're pulling one of those tricks where you correlate two completely unrelated things in a single piece in an attempt to make some obscure point." NOT THIS TIME. Birds, such as coots—which are actually and truly a type of bird—did not merely evolve from dinosaurs. They *are* dinosaurs. Newsweek.com says so, and it (the news, not newsweek.com) is awesome, so it must be true.

Now I'm no scientist, so I am the ideal person to explain this evolution thing to you. Dinosaurs roamed the earth millions of years before God came along and created it in seven days. Radiation seems like it was probably more of a thing back in dinosaur times, which could explain why their babies came out with all kinds of strange mutations that they passed on to their own children, and so on. Back plates, tail spikes, ugly toenails, you name it.

Then, Something Bad happened. It nearly destroyed life on this planet. We don't know what happened exactly, because we're more interested in the Apple Watch. Maybe an asteroid collided with Earth? Maybe volcanoes belched more garbage into the air than all sports radio talk shows combined? Maybe aliens needed to clear space for all the pyramids they wanted to build? Your scientific theory is as valid as any scientist's.

Nonetheless, Something Bad smeared out all the really badass dinosaurs, and the freakazoid ones who evolved feathers and hollow bones and tasty wings pulled through. Humans were not yet around to hardboil all their eggs, so now we coexist with the kakapo, which smells like honey and is so reproductively stunted that it will try to mate—unsuccessfully, to date—with humans.

If I had known before college that birds equal dinos, you would not be reading this book, as I would now be a professional ostrich farmer. But what does this bird-revelation mean to you, specifically?

It means that you have dinosaurs hurtling themselves at your freshly spring-cleaned windows. But the real significance runs even deeper. If the dinosaurs—who invented the words "mass extinction"—survived to the present day, then certainly we can survive whatever doomsday debacle dangles in the balance of gay marriage or steroids in baseball, but definitely not of the many looming global climate crises.

Whoops! I said the Dangerous Words sure to sic intellectuals and environmentalists on my case. Allow me to preempt their passionate arguments by stating that I feel completely assured that our very own climate crises present us no immediate threat. For instance, I read a recent headline in the *Durango Herald* that indicates we have—and I quote verbatim—"Plenty of Water." Furthermore, by venturing deep into the article's first sentence, I gathered that "In the southwest corner of the state [of Colorado], there should be enough water to serve the population through 2050."

Those with the greatest stakes in the matter—obviously, the manufacturers of daily desk calendars—have not yet calculated just how far away 2050 is. Until they do, I choose to live peacefully with the knowledge that I could die any day before 2050, so why stress myself into an early grave?

I selected the *Herald* article completely at random because it discusses the geographic portion of the United States where I lived at the time, and because it makes me feel okay about my foreseeable survival. But I could have selected any number of other sources from other places where the media fulfills its sacred duty to simultaneously inform and calm the general public.

In the interest of balance, though, let's hypothesize that one of these totally unpredictable cataclysmic events comes to pass, like a freak meteor collision or the oceans absorbing ninety percent of the heat of supposed global warming. What happens?

Heck if I know! If it happens, we can just blame the scientists for not fixing the problem before it escalated out of control. I have more pressing matters at hand, such as trademarking my own brand of Kentucky Fried Dino.

Aftermath

NOT TO TOOT MY OWN HORN, but I'm pretty much a math genius. Like, I scored more points on the SAT than any two teams have scored in a single Super Bowl *combined*, which means I'm worthy of a halftime show with performers way more famous than Katy Perry, whoever he is.

Other great math geniuses, like Grace Hopper and Benjamin Franklin, had to prove themselves to the rest of the world. But I never needed to publish a groundbreaking book or invent kites, let alone take a college math class. My intellect was free to study the humanities, which is where all the chicks are, anyway. And since then, it has been resting in a well-deserved hibernation state, awaiting its call to save the world.

That call came just the other day. I have been summoned to tutor a fifth grader struggling with math. Let's call her "Martha" to protect her identity, even though her name is Sophie.

Fifth grade math is kid's stuff to us whizzes. So I cruised right through "Martha's" homework, until I got to the actual mathy parts, and the fish jumped its tank. Her handout read less like a NASA flight plan and more like a doctoral dissertation on the hermeneutic aspects of the extant senatorial dockets of Caesar's early reign.

Which is to say: not a lot of numbers. The presence of words didn't exactly unnerve me. As a dual math/word prodigy, I was the rare kid in class who didn't stab myself with a mechanical pencil whenever we solved word problems such as the following:

> Jeb Bush leaves Philadelphia on an Amtrak train at 11:45 carrying eight apples. Chris Christie leaves New Orleans on a Union Pacific train at midnight carrying six million oranges. How many times will they forgotten by history before ~~Hillary Clinton~~ Oprah Winfrey announces what she's having for breakfast?

But "Martha's" problems contained neither transportation nor fruit. And the solutions they demanded were not absolutely correct numerical answers, also known as "the entire point of math." Instead, I had to "describe the relationship between the corresponding terms."

I was forced to deduce that, in my absence, they changed math.

The only "corresponding terms" I studied in fifth grade were part of the sexual education curriculum. And we were definitely not permitted to "describe their relationships." Which meant that's all we did at recess, because, pssh, we *so* knew, like, everything about "corresponding terms" from personal experience.

Gone are the Days of Yore, when you could ace a test with a concealed calculator. Calculators don't "describe" much of anything, except for those glorious calculator words like 80085.

I don't have kids of my own, or, for that matter, anyone else's. But if I did, I would not want them wasting time describing their thought processes—in their own words, no less! We really ought to start pawning children's math homework off on artificial intelligence, so that these kids can spend more of their time trying to explain to me what the heck is going on in *Minecraft*.

They might as well. By the time robots take over, literally every means of beneficial employment will be filled by an un-unionized worker who doesn't demand holidays, retirement, or ergonomics. And I say, good! We humans will have more time to sit around and enjoy a hearty laugh at the robots' expense, and they won't even realize it.

Understanding any humor more complex than the letters "lol" is beyond a robot's capacitors. They can't even understand sarcasm. When my cell phone falls into the toilet and I say, "Smooth move, ex-lax," my phone thinks I'm actually complimenting it.

You, on the other hand, are laughing at the many toilet-related layers to my razor-wire wit. That is, no offense, because you fart. Bodily functions are the font of all good chortles.

Sadly for them, Earth robots do not have any blunder in their busses. It's technically possible that robots will someday snicker at each other's oil seepages, but scientific studies probably show that robots will learn to turn water into wine, or wind and sun and geothermal activity into electricity, before they will truly comprehend gas being expelled from an orifice.

So you and your munchkins can pitch the hard work to the machines, relax, and enjoy some good ol' fashioned family bum-rumblers. To show your gratitude, you can talk to "Martha's" mother for me. She keeps calling about a tutoring refund, and that's the one mathematical calculation I'm no good at.

Presage Against the Machine

I LIKE TO KEEP ABREAST of what's happening in the world. That's why I try to examine magazine covers every time I'm in the grocery store checkout lane.

Hoo boy. Already I can envision the fan mail I will receive from the educated-at-a-college-that-doesn't-even-*have*-a-football-team crowd. They will ream me for collecting my news from the impulse-buy section. And then they will slyly inquire—you can practically hear them typing more quietly as they ask—whether the rumors about Lindsay Lohan and Tom Cruise are true.

Let me cut off all such correspondence by saying: I can't actually *read* the headlines in the checkout lane, no matter how hard I try. I'm always too stressed about bagging my own groceries because the stores don't hire enough baggers anymore. I remember you used to have two, even three young people prepared to stuff your canned vegetables atop your bread and bananas. They would gladly wheel your food to your car, where they would hurl it in the trunk and forget to wish you a nice day.

Such customer service is unheard of anymore, at least until someone invents a machine to forget to wish me a nice day. Until then, I'm left ruining my own groceries.

I now have reason to believe that such a glorious future may already be in the past. I discovered this at my public library where, unhurried by checkouts and surrounded by lifetimes of knowledge bound in sacred tomes, I can scour headlines in peace.

And *only* headlines, mind you. Magazines are vessels for advertisements, and thus to read a complete article is to expose oneself to subliminal commercial violation and also those really strong scratch-and-sniff perfume strips. Headlines have never misled me. They are pure, distilled journalism that gives me the straight facts without making me sneeze.

The headline that got me so excited was on a back issue of Popular Science: "Will Your Next Best Friend Be a Robot?"

It better be, if we want a much less socially awkward future!

Friendship hierarchies are *complicated*. We all know that dogs are our best friends. Yet whenever I tell a human friend that he is my next-best friend, my second fiddle, my solid Number Two, he gets all butt-hurt. A robot, however, will be programmed to return my texts even when it's mad at me.

I had to know more about the awesomeness of the future, so I tore through some more back issues. "The Future of the Car: How the Automobile Is Becoming More Than Just a Vehicle" promises that the copywriters at Popular Science know how to use a thesaurus effectively. It also declares that these conveyances are "Social, Self-Aware, Connected." I hope that means my roadster will actually add me back on Google+, which is still a thing, right?

But the same cover whispers, "People are gullible. Machines are smart. That's a problem." Um, hello? That's not a problem. It actually works completely in our favor if all smart machines turn out like Herbie the Love Bug, interested in lending a fender to the down-on-their-luck.

Yet the deeper I researched, the more I didn't think that was the case. A different issue declares, "The Next Frontier of Surveillance: Your Car." Friendly motorbuggies don't spy on you. This turn of headlines sounds like we have secretly returned to a terrible state of McCarthyism. (Get it? McCARthyism. It's like a Red Scare, only with wheels. A red sCARe, if you will.)

I jest, but only to soften the *really* bad news, like the "25 Reasons to Love Drones (and 5 Reasons to Fear Them)." As reason #1, the cover offers, "They'll soon be delivering your dinner." That leads to all kinds of shaky questions, such as: Is that a reason to love drones, or to fear them? Because a pizza delivery drone is not a teenager, am I morally obligated to tip it? Is five percent enough, or will that insult the drone and cause it to unfollow me?

Lest you think that the drone invasion is only someone else's problem—namely, mine—take this little tidbit into account: "Why Is Google Building a Robot Army?" Let me go on the official printed record here: I don't know, but I'm sure it's not simply to populate G+, nor to hunt down people who slam Google's innovative and revolutionary and definitely still relevant social network.

If Google's motive turns out to be evil, regular schmoes like us can "Defend Your Home with Artificial Intelligence." That's a great solution—if you're willing to put your next best friend *and* your motorcar in the line of fire. I'm not, which means civilization may be doomed. At least there will be a whole new form of life to populate the earth after all the humans are dead; I read that Tom and Lindsay may be getting serious.

Nippless

I FIND MYSELF THRILLED that *Playboy* has nipped the nip.

If you do not share the interests I have had since age fifteen **[Editor's note: Okay, twelve*]**, you may not have heard that *Playboy* magazine is joining the *Playboy* website and the Playboy Bunny icon itself in no longer revealing the female body in its entirety. There is, fortunately, nothing anyone can do to black-tape the magazines already under my mattress. But now, the Playboy brand will feature mere hints of nipples, rather than the nipples themselves.

At first, I could think of only a single positive outcome of this tragedy: one can theoretically now visit playboy.com on a public work computer without covering half the browser window with an Excel document. But the more my blood returned to my brain, the more I understood the great societal ramifications of this decision.

Yes! There are benefits to seeing less breast! I couldn't believe it either. But *Playboy*'s newfound modesty is going to help reinvent the American imagination.

---

*O-*kay*, ELEVEN.*

I know, I know; I write a lot of things that sound crack-potty until you stop reading them. But this one is blatantly true. Think about it. We everyday citizens live with our imaginative abilities being constant doubted. "Climate change will wreak unimaginable destruction." "You can't imagine a stricter gun bill passing Congress." "Can you imagine no possessions? John Lennon doesn't think you can."

No wonder our imaginations can't imagine anything: they get no emotional support whatsoever. We don't even get fresh new ideas at the movies; we get *Toy Story* turning into *The Land Before Time* with (seriously, I looked it up) twelve sequels AND COUNTING. **[Editor's note: As of press time, it's now fourteen total movies. Plus an animated series.]**

Who suffers? The children. They get their imaginative rights stripped away without even a plucky underdog's chance at rescuing them.

Case in point. There's this new Hello Barbie doll. Hello Barbie is like most dolls, in that she is slightly unnerving and she listens to a child's secrets. But Hello Barbie also has a microphone. Hello Barbie takes the child's stories—shared in confidence!—and beams them to some secret server hidden in the cloud. The server then tells Hello Barbie how to respond to the child.

First of all, the child will be traumatized when the Wi-Fi flickers out and this bestest of best fake friends goes dead. Second of all, you just *know* that older siblings will crash the secret cloud server by saying things to Hello Barbie that you could never even print in *Playboy*. Third through fifth of all, having a corporation eavesdrop on a child through a talking doll is, like, at least one and a half times scarier than Chucky.

But most relevant to the point is that this Hello Barbie-playing child will not use any ounce of imagination to give voice and life to Hello Barbie. The infinitely self-tailored possibilities are suddenly truncated to the eight thousand or so responses Hello Barbie knows. I would bet the farm—any farm, you choose—that Hello Barbie does not know how to console a child spilling the story of her irritable bowel syndrome acting up on the playground. Game over.

That child's imagination would do a better job giving voice to what the kid needs to hear. Hell, I just used my own imagination to invent a scenario that the folks at Mattel either didn't consider or won't dare touch. Imagination for the win.

And this brings us back to *Playboy*. I seriously love boobs and other such parts of the female anatomy. I want to look at high-quality photographs of them. *Playboy* wanted to show them. This was a win-win. But *Playboy*'s success extended beyond my visual pleasures. I think the magazine, through its quality articles and good old-fashioned objectification of women, helped liberate all genders of people from a bit of our own prudishness.

The proof is in the puddin', as they say. Boobs are so acceptable now that it is no longer profitable to show them.

But do we connoisseurs get tired of boobs? No! Do we pass on an opportunity to have anything at all to do with them? *Hell* no! We still want them. We just ... well, we want to have to *work* for them.

Whenever we don't want to work for them, they are a mere "turn off SafeSearch" away. But the imagination is a powerful draw: *Playboy*'s website traffic has quadrupled since it slipped into something more comfortable.

I mean it. I think all of us human animals really do want to use our imaginations. And not just for nudie pictures—we want to imagine ways of protecting the environment, and improving the quality of human life, and exploring space, and pirating televised sporting events because we don't have cable.

Through its newfound application of scant clothing, *Playboy* is stimulating creative faculties as much as it has always stimulated other faculties. Playmate nipples can finally be whatever we need them to be! And no one can tell you how to imagine. Not even Hello Barbie. Nips are remarkably not in her repertoire.

[Editor's note: *Playboy* reinstated the nip, and then some. We will ask the author for comment when he starts leaving the house again. Until such time, please disregard this entry in *Call Me Zach Hively Because That Is My Name*.]

Bruin up
Halloween Trouble

THINK ABOUT WHAT A HOLIDAY REALLY MEANS. It's a sacred time for celebrating togetherness, or giving thanks, or buying affection with chocolate and grossly oversized teddy bears.

Not Halloween. Halloween is a big phony masquerading as a holiday. This night, more than any night, is about being strangers. The best costume is one where even your friends don't recognize you, or better yet, they genuinely believe you are someone else. We can be anyone, repercussion-free. It's like identity theft with candy.

The whole ordeal doesn't tax our higher thinking with abstract concepts like "peace on Earth" and "love" and "how to keep the turkey moist." Instead, Halloween speaks the language of adrenaline, sugar, and sex. We scare ourselves silly. We threaten our neighbors with vandalism unless they hand over their best candy, and after they tell us we're too old to be doing that anymore, we crash parties where we flirt with the sexy nurse/pirate/ninja/mechanic who would normally not even notice us, but not tonight, because it's really difficult to ignore the person in the screen-quality Darth Vader suit.

Despite all the wholesome fun, Halloween has no revered saint or secular hero. So I propose a stand-alone totem for the occasion, a creature all about massive amounts of food and terror, a monster that will really cause me to soil myself:

Bears.

Not cutesy T-shirt-wearing and honey-pot-pilfering bears, either. I'm talking the musky, rippled, sprints-faster-than-a-horse, chows-twenty-thousand-calories-a-day beast of the forest.

Yeah, yeah, some of you may be snickering at my continued—and well-earned—bear caution. *Garbage bins and apple trees have more to fear from our ursine residents than trick-or-treaters do,* you mutter. But those of you laughing haven't learned what I learned by listening to Anne Bryant, the executive director of the Bear League in Tahoe, California.

Bryant talked to NPR about bears breaking into cars. The bears aren't tearing through convertible tops or snaking clothes hangers through door seals. No, the bears open the cars using the door handles. How, you ask?

They have learned by spying on us.

"Bears are evolving faster than humans are," Bryant said, "and they're taking over."

Those words bear repeating, because they were spoken by a genuine bear expert: BEARS ARE TAKING OVER.

I'm a city boy by birth. Wildlife, in my view, is a dog running around without a leash. Things changed for me when I moved to a mountain town in Colorado. Yet I proved I was a natural survivalist when my first-ever Durango bear encounter ended with one of us dashing into the safety of the woods, and the other casually riding away on my bicycle.

People keep telling me that bears really are interested in leaving me alone, that so long as I don't threaten them they won't threaten me. All I know is that surviving an encounter with a startled bear made me feel pretty badass. Unlike my bike, no one could take that away from me.

No one, that is, until one little offhand remark from a longtime resident of bear country explained the politics of the local food chain:

"Give the bear your candy."

What? Like, leave the bowl of Skittles outside on Halloween night?

"No. If a bear comes sniffing after your candy while you're trick-or-treating, drop the bag and leave it."

Okay, I dealt with the threat of bag-snatchers growing up. But even the ones who were big and hairy for their age wouldn't actually eat me just to get to my candy.

Yet the bears are not stopping at cars and Halloween candy. Oh no. They are going after the creamy and/or chunky core of all that America stands for. According to Bryant, "They have learned how to open peanut butter jars. Whereas ten years ago they'd smash them to get the peanut butter inside, now they simply turn the lid off."

Bears are infiltrating our lives where communism and *American Idol* both fell short. I know actual human beings who can't unscrew a peanut butter lid. And most of them have thumbs. Uncapping peanut butter jars is one of the hallmarks of evolved intelligence, along with dumpster diving and stealing bicycles.

There's one thing in common between all those activities: humans taught bears to do them. (Unless it's the other way around. But let's not consider such a horror.)

Carelessness in opening car doors and Jif jars in full view of peeping bruins has brought about the evolution of genius bears. They are our Frankenstein's monsters. Heaven help us when they learn to speak French and open the Welch's grape.

Humans are the devices of our own undoing. That's why even on Halloween, the night of living irresponsibly, we have to recognize our duties to the natural world. While we're cavorting about with our reptilian brains in charge, we can still consider the repercussions of our actions. Are any bears watching you unwrap that Mars bar?

Failure to consider the consequences means we'll end up with real monsters—and this time, human carelessness is the slasher in the house. So keep monsters at bay this Halloween. Make certain your toilet paper is biodegradable when you go TPing, and ensure that your egging missiles are free-range and hormone-free. And if you truly want to scare some folks tonight, dress up as our cousin in evolution: the bear. The musky scent might keep you from winning the sexy nurse/pirate/ninja/mechanic, but you'll definitely score some candy.

Catatonic Water

FOR HALLOWEEN, SOME PEOPLE WENT in costume. Me? I went to bed.

And can you blame me? There are so many reasons to be tired. It's go-go-go all day long, working and grocery shopping and playing with the more interactive Google doodles. Plus, this time of year there's the extra effort of hiding from the election volunteers knocking on my door. I need some serious rest and relaxation, and this weekend's bonus hour of turn-back-the-clock sleep just won't cut it.

There's no way that my mind will truly chill out until the upcoming election is done and dusted. Meanwhile, I see no reason why my body can't relax. So I decided to go to the local hot springs for the very first time.

Why not? Nothing says "relaxation" like slipping into a pool of hot water—water that stains the earth the full color spectrum of a 1980s San Diego Padres jersey—with a dozen or so strangers. But hey, at least they're not naked!

I figured no nudity was a given. I mean, we're not in some exotic European backwater here. But plenty of posted signage around the facilities reminds you to wear a swimsuit because your body is a shameful slab of flesh that no one wants to look at, unless one is a perv or you are really hot.

Now if there is one place in this country where all different kinds of people could go naked, these hot springs seem like the place. We are already submerging our nakedness bits in the same pools of water. Breathing the same steamy sauna air. Stepping on the same dressing room floor when my foot snags on my underwear and I lose my balance just a little bit and I don't get my bare foot back in my flip-flop fast enough. There's really not much else for us to share. Could I actually pick up any more contamination through my eyeballs?

This being the United States of America, the answer is "Hellz yes I could. I am fine absorbing all you strangers and your shared bodily slough through my skin and my nostrils. That, I can rationalize away, or ignore. But I durst not absorb the image of your nudity through my eyeholes into my soul, where it might—nay, where it *wouldst*—taint my fragile virtue."

Don't blame this repressive opinion on me. I'm merely thinking the thoughts of my culture. And if this is our cultural opinion of the human body—which, let's be honest, it is—then it's small wonder that my own needs some soothing care and healing warmth in what is, essentially, volcano spit.

I'm hardly hyperbolizing. There's water underground, toasting itself atop the earth's molten belly. The earth hocks it back up like a sulfuric loogie. And then we take baths in it.

Neverminding the obvious conclusion that we are seated atop a potential eruption, it's pretty friggin' empowering to soak in volcano saliva. Or maybe that's just me, since I love volcanoes. I'm basically a volcano expert. Everything I know about volcanoes, I made up as a kid while drawing dinosaurs. Volcanoes were everywhere in dinosaur times, and they were always erupting. You couldn't sneak past an Eodromaeus without stepping on an exploding volcano. If volcanoes are like the earth's zits, only awesomer, then the prehistoric earth looked like my face at fourteen.

But where Clearasil still doesn't do the trick for me, the earth has cleared its skin right up. It has only the occasional stress breakout in places like Hawai'i. And if these hot springs are as relaxing as advertised, maybe they'll do a thing or two for my own complexion.

Yet it was with no such hopes of miracle cures that I dipped into the steaming tub on a clear autumnal afternoon. I just wanted to relax for a few minutes, ease away my tension, and leave feeling lighter, running faster, and jumping higher.

Even so, I realized right away that this place was truly removed from the world. Here, no one was talking about the election, because no one was talking, period. No errands to run. No to-do lists, no niggling work assignments. No looming apocalypses. No judgmental cultural norms making me shield my man-nips from public view. All there was, was ... patience.

I could bob in these pools and heal myself for as long as I wanted, or until closing time, or until I couldn't take it anymore because the water is really hot. But I was on my own sched. No one else could tell me what to do, dammit. I gifted my body the warmth of the earth and a break from time.

Now, with my newfound relaxation, I'm going to sleep like Rip Van Winkle. Please don't wake me up until it's all over.

Stuffed

THANKSGIVING IS THE ONE PURE North American holiday, free ~~of politics of commercialism~~ of historical accuracy. Most people like to celebrate the warm-and-fuzzy animal sacrifice side of Thanksgiving. And that's fine; America is nothing if not a nation of moderation, so we should be allowed one single meal of overindulgence each year.

But what many don't realize is that Thanksgiving was not founded on comfort food, closed retail stores, and the Detroit Lions losing. The holiday's roots are much more sinister than that. If *Thanksgiving: The Origins* were a Netflix original series, it would be shot entirely in black, there would be lots of Meaningful Expressions, all your favorite characters would die, and you would be thankful that there was no Season Two.

The historical time we romanticize as the First Thanksgiving was but one instance of the most dreaded circumstance known to mankind, not counting impending genocide, which was also a factor. These gritty, dramatic, white pilgrims had packed up their worldly belongings and relocated to a strange new land. When they arrived, they had no food to eat, nor plates to eat food from, because everything they owned was still packed in moving boxes.

This predicament was not the pilgrims' choice. No one chooses to move gladly. The original Thanksgiving pilgrims probably liked England a lot; they liked it so much, in fact, that they kept naming American places after English ones, like Norwich and Worcheseshestersheshire. But they had to move because the English wanted to get rid of all their stodgiest religious types.

I am likewise a modern-day pilgrim. I am being persecuted out of my home by landlords who are selling this house so they—and this is the problem with capitalism—can move closer to their grandchildren. I'm searching for a new home where I would be willing to bathe without wearing shower shoes. Until then, I'm packing all my worldly possessions, which if you don't think about it too much is a lot like sailing across the Atlantic Ocean in a wooden vessel, only without the luxury views.

With all my belongings packed away, I'm too exhausted from thinking about moving to dig through boxes for my Thanksgiving cookware, or a spoon for cereal.

Not coincidentally, I am commemorating Thanksgiving in my house in the truest spirit of the festival: by eating peanut butter sandwiches on a table made of cardboard.

This sort of predicament is exactly what the pilgrims faced. Left alone, they would have starved before they figured out which box held their Crock-Pot. Heck, they didn't even know for sure where they'd packed their full-length pantaloons or the buckles for their tennis shoes.

You can often tell that one is moving just by examining one's clothing. The functional wardrobe of a typical human being is repurposed during a move: socks pad fragile chachkies, coffee mugs are mummy-wrapped in underwear, and dress pants function nicely as furniture blankets. So one wears whatever combination of dish towels and house slippers one can successfully locate until the boxes are unpacked or one moves again, whichever happens first. In fact, little-known historical tidbit: the pilgrims strapped belts to their hats because they could not find where they packed all their elastic hat bands.

Fortunately for most of us, our moving-year outfits are not immortalized in elementary school historical recreations. But wardrobe oddities are not even the most challenging part of moving. There's also that long, slow realization of how much extraneous stuff you have in your possession. That is not the most challenging part, either, but it's the part I want to talk about.

I went into this round of moving with the mindset that I would pare down all unnecessary belongings and live a simpler life for it. But then packing up this old place took longer than the three hours I had budgeted for it, so I've ended up stuffing everything in cardboard boxes, canvas bags, suitcases, shopping carts, the glovebox in the car, and my pockets. I can hardly imagine how the Mayflower looked with miscellaneous coat hangers poking out of every hold.

Now I'd like you to ponder the stereotypical, traditional, modern Thanksgiving for just a moment. Imagine the dining room. Do you envision even a single box with Sharpie scrawl graffitied on the side?

No—because the true spirit of Thanksgiving is being grateful that, wherever you are, you are not moving. So please, when you give thanks around the table, remember those of us less fortunate. And if you feel compelled by white guilt to lend a hand, please find someone more deserving of help than I am.

Derby Is
My Jam

WHEN I ATTENDED A DURANGO ROLLER GIRLS roller derby bout, my friend—let's call him "Tim" because that is his name—and I had very different experiences. For my own part, I have to say that it was a relief to watch a sport where I as an audience member don't objectify the participants. Unlike, say, football.

I've really gotten turned off of football, and it's not because of the NFL's unwillingness to tackle the long-term effects of head injuries, or the slogging minutes of nothing happening between marathons of commercials. No, what gets my goat is that Americans tune in to football so they can goggle over the glorified male physiques on display while ignoring the athleticism, dedication, and detection-evading performance enhancing drugs that these athletes bring to every game.

We reduce these individuals to their position on the field, their artificially enhanced shoulders and quads, and a last name on their jerseys. We forget that these men have college degrees and childhood traumas, mistresses and drug addictions all their own. They are not mere slabs of meat with regional logos on their heads.

Derby girls, on the other hand, are impossible for me to reduce to their physical bodies. That's not to say these women don't have phenomenal physiques. They're athletes, after all, and Tim understandably defaulted to viewing them just like football players. Perhaps I too could appreciate their sculpted frames if I weren't so invested in the nuances of skating, strategy, and whatever the hell else is going on out there during the game-jam-competition thingy.

Tim wanted to know how I enjoy this sport without reducing the participants to pinups, and here's how I explained it: these derby girls are whole human beings with the full spectrum of their selves on display, augmented only with pragmatic sporting equipment like fishnets and tattoos and high socks. Oh, and roller skates. Speaking for myself here, I cannot focus on lesser superficial aspects when there's so much more to these women.

Also, unlike those objectionally objectifiable professional footballers, these women are everyday people like me and, presumably, you. They are bankers, therapists, EMTs, administrative assistants, and marijuana retailers. Like I said, just everyday folk, with everyday names like Eager Beaver and Mutha Stucka and Quadess of Pain and Illegal Peaches.

But—and I cannot stress this enough—that's the end of where these women are like the rest of us. Put wheels on their feet, and they turn into superhumans. Also unlike the rest of us, these ladies are truly well-rounded people. You can tell just by observing.

Throughout the night, Tim and I discussed just how well developed they are as individuals. Certainly they discuss philosophy, recite poetry, and repair automobiles. Without a doubt, they're philanthropists; they're probably seeding money for the next natural disaster before whatever current one is even finished. We wondered what they're like in bedlam—they are undoubtedly level-headed under duress.

And we concluded they must be really good at giving heads-up notices to their business associates when derby schedules conflict with work commitments.

But that was just two men getting carried away, day-dreaming about the fullness of these women's personalities. For the hour and a half they're on wheels, none of those qualities matter to the derby girls. All that counts is the competition. They channel all their passions quite fiercely into it.

As for all the other diverse and well-developed qualities these roller girls bring to the rink, it's their badassery at roller derbying that is most obviously and undeniably blatant. It ill behooves me to ignore this facet of their stunning characters. To truly appreciate these women and their accomplishments, we made certain to appreciate the skills they were practicing right before our very eyes.

I don't wish to single out any one player, so I won't identify whose skills Tim and I studied in greatest depth throughout the match-bout-contest whatsit. One might think one would overlook this player because her name doesn't rhyme with one of the more popularly censored phrases in our vernacular. But during any particular scrum-tangle-block-event, she uses her skills so deftly—so gracefully, in fact—that one could only acknowledge that "oh, *those* are her peaches."

And that's why ... wait, what was I driving toward?

Oh yeah. A conclusion. To be honest, I expected to reach an understanding of our deeper humanity by this point. Something that connected my roller derby experience with an intrinsic truth about decency and respect. But such growth was not for me; I entered the rink already able to value human beings for who they are, without resorting to judgment on superficial levels.

But I was fortunate to be able to aid Tim in expanding his myopic focus and appreciating our local derby girls as profoundly talented human beings. Next season, we will be rinkside for every home bout-joust-round, in hopes that one of them will flash us her real name and invite us out for an intellectual conversation.

The Greatest Story Ever Told

I AM A FAN OF NATIONAL TREASURES reclaiming their original names. Like when President Obama returned Denali to its Native name, dropping the stage name "Cougar" for good. The Mount Formerly Known as McKinley sparked all kinds of political controversy, such as who exactly McKinley was, and how much more he represents America than Lincoln, Washington, and hot dogs combined.

Controversy aside, I think that returning original names to great landmarks is an effective and creative way to preserve our national heritage. After all, so many moral problems would have been averted if Miley Cyrus had simply remained Hannah Montana.

But to restore traditional monikers, we must first understand our ancient heritage. To learn more, I turned to my little sister Kara, who is studying claymation at the University of New Mexico, which means she's an authoritative expert on folktales.

I recently roped her into my renaming crusade. She offered me plenty of examples of New Mexico folklore. These include stories like "Coyote Sleeps with His Own Daughters" and "The Toothed Vagina." While these tales promise rich clues to the origins of place names, they might prove difficult to garner popular support for a renaming effort. My mission requires legends with the trifecta of 1) staying power, 2) general appeal, and 3) imagery that's evocative but less so than dentured genitalia.

Thank goodness my little sister also shared the tale of "Monster Skunk Farting Everyone to Death." This story is really real, or else a convincing forgery elaborated by third graders. The title says it all. Even so, the story is worth retelling here, because it is in the public domain. Here goes:

MONSTER SKUNK FARTING EVERYONE TO DEATH

Monster Skunk was killing everyone by farting on them. After cooking them in his Dutch oven, he ate them.

This one whole village, which should probably be renamed in honor of these events, freaked out because Monster Skunk was coming right for them. They ran around like it was Black Friday and only the first twenty customers could buy survival.

So after a series of committee meetings, Bobcat and Coyote decided they would kill Monster Skunk, who was as big as Godzilla only instead of knocking down buildings he basically only farted a lot.

Meanwhile, the people listening to this story around the campfire wanted to hear more about Monster Skunk before he died. So, using the Storytelling Rule of Threes, Monster Skunk encountered three men on the road.

The first man was afraid of Monster Skunk farting, so Monster Skunk farted him to death. The second man was afraid of Monster Skunk defecating, so in a plot twist, Monster Skunk defecated him to death. And the third one built his house of bricks, but Monster Skunk blew it down anyway with his spray and he skunked the man to death.

Then Monster Skunk chased a woman who was really interested in providing landmarks to be named after this folktale. She turned her possessions into a forest, a mountain, and most impressively of all, a hedge. But Monster Skunk farted right through these obstacles, and then he farted the woman—seriously, it's in the story—to pieces.

Then the storyteller really wanted to prove to me how badly my public school education lacked valuable traditional knowledge. A grandmother and her granddaughter played dead to fool Monster Skunk. Monster Skunk bought their act, but only because he mistook their genitalia for knife wounds, which just goes to show how little even mythological men know what they're actually talking about in the realm of women's reproductive rights.

Finally, Monster Skunk stumbles upon Bobcat's and Coyote's ambush. Lo—they cannot kill the Monster Skunk! Then Coyote remembers the successful conclusion of the Death Star battle in *Star Wars*. Monster Skunk's thermal exhaust port is only two meters wide, but Coyote is clever enough to turn off her targeting computer. Using the Force, she jams a boulder up Monster Skunk's port.

Coyote and Bobcat book it far, far away. The village is in Monster Skunk's firing range, but he's completely backed up. He grunts, and he groans, and he clenches, and at the final desperate moment he explodes. He literally farts himself to death.

The village people hold a celebratory feast, at which they decide the main course should be hunks of farting skunk, because this reciprocal act will hold great symbolic meaning for future anthropologists. They gift Bobcat and Coyote the best parts, which in my mind would be two tickets out of town.

THE END

And now I don't have any idea what my original point was. But I sure hope that someone will take swift action to address it.

Trolls of Yuletide Carols

LAST YEAR, I JOURNALISMED AN EXPOSÉ on the Krampus. He's this man-goat-demon who accompanies ol' St. Nick and whips the naughty children. No one, by which I mean me, had ever heard of him, because contemporary mothers generally don't approve of an eel-tongued creature scaring their children so severely that they don't sleep for a month. But once I unveiled him for the world, Krampus lost his chompers. Now, even everyday people like you can make Krampus cards for Christmas.

You'll never hear me say this again, so take note: I was wrong. I should not have limelighted the Krampus. He is just a front to cover up an even nastier demon running among us.

This foul beast will break into a home without necessarily obtaining a warrant. And then it will interrogate you. If it thinks you are being uncooperative, it will sit you on a cold concrete floor without pants. Yet, if you are forthright with fabricating information, it will crave even *more* answers. Therefore, it will coax you with rectal feeding and waterboarding.

Wait—that's the CIA. Hah! Thank goodness you can count on those folks to laugh off an honest mistake. They must have been on my mind because so many whiny wusses, like Congress, are all upset about the CIA's intense desire to protect our right to apathy. But because secret agents haven't interrogated me personally, I'm not that ruffled.

Besides, those fine folks keep us safe from foreign invaders who want to destroy our way of life. Invaders like our Christmas demon of the moment, the Belsnickel.

The Belsnickel smuggled itself aboard the Mayflower, the famous ferry upon which all immigrants traveled to America until we invented border fences. It hid itself from the World At Large in a cave deep in the Appalachians. I know this, because I read a website that taught me everything I needed in order to become the World's Leading Expert.

Since prehistoric times, the Belsnickel has wandered into private homes to quiz children on memorized verses, multiplication tables, and how to "log up" to this confounded "internet thing." You want to talk harsh techniques? Wrong or poor answers warrant a switch-wuppin'. Correct answers earn candy strewn on the ground; but, if children grab the candy, they get a switch-wuppin'. If at any other point the Belsnickel feels like it, children get a switch-wuppin'.

However, even I, the World's Leading Expert, have some eensy bit o' brain space left to fill with fresh knowledge. For instance, I don't have a good read on the Belsnickel's appearance because the National Science Foundation won't approve my grant to research it. What I do know is that it is vaguely human-shaped and wears a nondescript mound of fur. It may also have placed one year in the Westminster dog show, unless that was a Newfoundland. (The existing photos are inconclusive.)

I for one do not want this beast tromping into my compatriots' homes and terrorizing their children. Given the choice between an Unquestionable Good and a Ruthless Investigator who metes out baseless punishments, any upstanding American would choose the CIA. Especially at

Christmastime. But thanks to the happy Krampus hysteria I might have maybe unwittingly triggered, folks are too busy hot-gluing sequins and tassels to Krampus's anatomy to consider proper home and/or Christmas defense.

If I don't stand up for Christmas in every home from sea to oil-slicked sea, Christmas as the Magi intended it and America perfected it, then no one will.

I didn't ask for this burden. I preferred living blissfully unaware of the world's dangers, believing we were safe as houses—which, I learn as I grow older and more handsome, are not exactly safe. Like, at all.

Let me gift you two holiday examples of distinctly unsafe houses:

- A man in Catoosa County, Georgia, had his house mercilessly burned to the ground by a turkey. In the turkey's defense, it was being deep-fried in the man's garage. But that cannot overshadow the fact that your house is also flammable, no matter how macho your means of cooking your bird.

- In a more chilling example of mayhem, I fought a wall, and the wall won. All I did was bend down to unplug a strand of Christmas lights, and next thing I knew, the doorjamb punched me in the face. I still pretend to have the scar on my brow as proof of how vindictive even a rental apartment can get.

See what I mean? If hearth and home remain unsecure, then nothing will stop civilization from collapsing every December into the Belsnickel's realm of primal thrills. Words of ancient songs we've never understood, like "wassailing" and "figgy pudding," will crawl from their graves. No one will work for a week or more. The rich will serve the poor, and the poor will reign supreme. We will have uncontrolled mirth, abundance, and drinking in the streets!

Hold on. That actually sounds pretty enticing. Where do I sign up?

To the Dogs

MY LOCAL HUMANE SOCIETY RUNS a no-kill shelter, which is the most compassionate way to treat the poor, helpless volunteers. If lives were truly in the balance, someone would be sure to jailbreak every death row inmate in direct violation of someone's new lease and someone's shoe collection, which would be tragic, because it takes a lot of years to break in a pair of tennis shoes the way someone wants them.

This shelter policy means I can feel free to volunteer with the dogs at will. Doing so is a selfless way to fill my unconditional-love quota without any of the actual responsibilities of pet ownership. You play with them, get them all wound up, then return them to their cages. Just like unclehood.

The first thing I noticed my first day at the humane society—and the awe still lingers—is that the kennel does not smell, pardon my Finnish Lapphund, like dog poop. These shelter people do a stellar job of keeping the place clean.

I was promptly volunteer-oriented, and then I was handed a plastic shopping bag and a dog on a leash. Zarya would make a sweet family companion, if any dearest reader is looking, cough cough. She doesn't attack other walkers on the river trail, and she is fully housetrained. She's so well trained, in fact, that she will not stop'n'squat until she reaches a reasonable distance from the last trash can on the walking path.

Zarya grinned at me as she plied her craft. She believed she was a Good Girl. Apparently, the secret to maintaining kennel cleanliness is to sucker volunteers into taking dogs for long walks with plastic baggies.

Now I had a Sophie's Choice before me. Leaving this deposit on the side of the trail would reflect poorly on the shelter and on the honor of my volunteer badge. Picking it up would mean carrying a Fukushima time bomb for the last twenty-four minutes of our half-hour walk with nothing but a veneer of Walmart plastic keeping me sanitary.

What I chose is not important. What is important is that, after volunteering at least two times now, I still don't know how the shelter staff determine the breeds of the dogs.

This is especially true of the mutts and *especially* true of the puppies. I suspect the staff skim the "List of dog breeds most desired by suckers" Wikipedia page, and they pick one or two of these, and they add the word "mix" as a catch-all butt-cover.

Incidentally, this is why most dogs, even Chihuahuas, are lab/shepherd mixes. My mother adopted a lab/shepherd mix as a puppy, and she (the dog, not my mother) is now a Great Dane.

Anyway, when I got tired of carrying warm hand grenades on walks, I took a look at a puppy who was remarkably not a lab/shepherd mix. She was a border collie. You know, just to switch things up.

The puppy—let's call her Moore, because the shelter did—was ten weeks old. Her siblings, Mary and Tyler, had found homes during the shelter's Black Friday adoption special, an event for people who want to have to feed their gifts for a full month before Christmas. I sincerely hope these people poke holes in the boxes.

Somehow this little sweetums, whose paws were still just the size of pancakes and who barked only when she didn't have a human's fullest attention, had not been adopted the entire holiday weekend. So I asked to play with her in the socialize-with-puppies room.

Yes, playing with puppies is an actual thing you can volunteer to do *for FREE*. People pay a ton of money to do this at home! At the peril of their own carpet!

Granted, "play" is a relative term. At ten weeks, Moore had already grasped the nuances of fetch. But tug o' war was out, and she was oblivious to the subtleties of I spy. "Play" largely meant "ignore the human and interact with the broom instead."

There's absolutely no accounting for taste.

Such a strange puppy. Yet after the first hour together, my perspective melted. Moore was not choosing the broom in lieu of me. She was merely independent. And how many games had I mastered by ten weeks of age? Nothing more complex than Uno.

Was ... was I falling for Moore? Could I even consider taking her home? I had chosen volunteering over adoption in no small part because the yard at my new home is unenclosed ever since a bear sat on the fence until it broke.

When Moore tuckered out, she flopped on my leg, all cute and manipulative. The shelter staff kept asking me heavily if I loved her yet.

Once more, what I chose is not important. What is important is that Moore found a home before I made my decision. And she inspired me to start stockpiling plastic bags for any future canine companions. You cannot ever trust that no one is watching.

Litter
Wonderland

ALRIGHT. WE HERE AT *CALL ME ZACH HIVELY Because That Is My Name* are back in business after a long winter's nap, only minus the nap. You see, the season has another long-standing, or long-lying, tradition that I've had to deal with instead of snoozing.

Most such traditions have to do with the clump of holidays we just survived. Some people seize this time to slip into heavy drinking, others into meth. I, on the other hand, slip on ice.

This year, I traveled for a week to visit family, and when I came home, I discovered that municipal street-plowing services do not extend to personal front yards. Faced with so much frozen runoff, I could have beaten myself silly against the forces of nature. But I didn't. I simply resigned myself to living with an icy stoop until it melts oh around June. Better that the ritual slipping-on-the-ice happen at my own front door than out in public, captured on security camera footage.

Yet even though the ice in places was no thicker than a Chicago deep dish, I was expecting Pops to come visit for the new year. And I figured he might like to have his tailbones unbroken for the duration of his stay.

To stave off his slippage, I purchased my very first bag of rock salt. I sprinkled it along my iced walkway. And then I read my very first rock salt bag label.

The repercussions of coming into incidental contact with rock salt sound more severe than dying on ice. Plus, the salt could really erode the vibe of my shoes.

So I turned to alternative means. Sand is good for traction—think of how nobody falls down in the opening shots of *Baywatch*—but I was already going to the grocery store, which does not sell sand, but which *does* sell kitty litter.

Now I know very little about cats. I know they are warm and cuddly in one's lap while they tease their claws through one's pants and into one's genitals. I know they wear their buttholes like merit badges. And I know at least one real Coloradan who carries kitty litter in the trunk to gain traction on snowy roads.

So I bought a box of kitty litter, and I sprinkled it atop my rock-salted porch, and within a few magical hours, it all turned to mush.

I don't know if you have ever tried to clean kitty litter oatmeal off of wet pavement, but if you have, you probably failed, too. Pops showed up, and our first order of business was to rid our feet of kitty litter hash. Thus, we went snow-shoeing.

To be perfectly honest, I didn't believe snowshoeing would so much as clear the tread in my boots. My under-standing of the molecular physics behind the sport is that you strap tennis racquets to your feet and Jesus around the new-fallen snow, remaining perfectly dry. But, hey, at this point, if my two racquets were strung with the guts of actual kitty-litter manufacturers, I'd call it even.

No such luck. We rented poles and metal shoes, which looked like they wouldn't even be allowed on the grounds at Wimbledon. As nimbly as I could with what felt like a small child clutching each ankle, I clopped deftly, even expertly, atop the first snowdrift along the trail. And I promptly clopped—deftly, most definitely expertly—knee-deep into it.

That's right. One does not, technically, walk on top of snow in snowshoes. The legend of snowshoes is a fabrication, dear children—a lie perpetrated by parents and society to keep us enthralled until really you ought to have figured it out by now and it's kind of embarrassing, actually, to admit to our friends that you still believe in it.

But, Pops had paid for the shoes until six o'clock, so we trudged ever deeper into the forest, pausing only to turn around at the halfway point, a process which, in snowshoes, would be aided by a railway turntable. While taking a breather, I stabbed my poles straight down in the snow, and they disappeared up to the hilt.

Welp. We were standing a mere eight inches deep atop perhaps four feet of powder. These snowshoes are no religious experience, mind you, but they appeared to be actually keeping us afloat.

I really got the hang of those things on the way out of the woods. The mountain air rejuvenated my spirits, and whaddya know, the snow cleansed my shoes of cat litter.

We came home happy, and then my front porch directly re-littered our shoes. But right now, I have zero energy to clean them again. Snowshoeing is way too exhausting, and I still haven't had that nap.

Making Waves

MY LATEST LIFELONG PASSION involves fulfillment of my true nature's potential. Also, science! You see, the gravitational waves that Einstein proposed back inna day explain so much about my ability to do yoga.

Now when I say "my ability to do yoga," I am not trying to make you feel bad about your own inabilities. My yoga teacher says that we yogis are not to judge our stupid inflexible bodies. We are all built differently, she says, which is the absolute nicest way anyone has ever shamed connective tissues.

You see, some people's abilities are as invisible as gravitational waves. But it's not invisibility that explains my yogic accomplishments; it's the way gravitational waves collaborate with my body to render majestically complex poses.

Bear in mind, I don't pretend to understand the advanced science behind gravitational waves—I genuinely *do* understand them. The trick here is to find an image or a metaphor that illustrates the challenging concept to other people. This tactic is what we in the journalism biz refer to as "using our advanced training, for once," or "I told you an English degree wasn't completely worthless, Pops."

You, dear reader, will be aided by an evocative image, like this: The way a gravitational wave works is, it pulls objects to the earth quicker than a pantser can expose the fruits of their victim's looms.

Before this discovery of gravitational waves, gravity was a mere theory, untested and unobservable, like evolution and bipartisanship. Now that scientists have detected gravitational waves for realsies, though, I have science to verify my triumphs on the yoga mat.

Like many other, more normal, people, I assumed for years that yoga was not for me. I should never have listened to myself. Yoga is a powerful spiritual activity, traditionally harmonizing the physical body with the ethereal reality of failure. But not for me. For me, on Day One, there was only mastery.

To be fair, my excellent teacher deserves her share of the credit. She explained, in a soothing voice, that this is a yin yoga class, where we work with gravity to create sensation in the body. So I, as a great understander of gravitational waves, was already starting light years ahead of everyone else. As part of yin yoga, she continued, we hold each pose for three to five minutes.

Too easy, drill sergeant. I squirmed through many years of my sisters' middle school band concerts. After those, I'm not afraid of three to five minutes of *anything*.

The teacher first reclined us into a simple pose—let's just call it Regurgitated Butterfly—and it all went to plan as I surrendered my groin to gravity.

The real secret of gravity is that it never lets up. Its wavelengths expand or contract when there are cosmic shifts in the density of matter, like when two black holes merge, or when Associate Justice Antonin Scalia passed away. But gravity. never. stops. pulling. on. your. groin.

As a man, I have learned to keep my pain to myself. So I applied the same principle to my non-pain. I strove to breathe through it, like my teacher suggested. She must have recognized my significant abilities, because she heaped praise on me before everyone else.

She was all, *I'm going to help you ease your knees apart into the pose, alright?* And I was all, *I can't acknowledge you because I'm focused on breathing like a yoga master*. And she was all, *Just go as far as you are comfortable*, and I was all, *Okay*, and that's when she talked about us each being built differently.

When the teacher moved the class into the next pretzel-pose, she once again came over to me and was like, *Normally we save Corpse Pose until the end, but why don't you go ahead and give it a try*.

I was the first to the finish line! And Corpse Pose is truly relaxing. It reflects a person who died peacefully, even tranquilly, from kicking ass in yoga class.

When the hour ended, I must admit I felt somewhat ... less gravitied. While everyone else was busy attempting the Caucused Wombat and the Ever-Stubborn Sloth, I grew metaphysically, merging my being with gravity waves and reaching self-actualization.

This yoga thing is so worth another week of lifelong practice. My teacher helped me detect my true nature right away. Who knows what else I will learn from her. Perhaps she is a yogic Einstein who understands potentials that I cannot even imagine. If she is reading this now, she should know that her gentle instruction led my chakras and my meridians spiritually far, far beyond Kapotasana pose, so I should never ever have to attempt it. Pretty please?

Dialed Up

DESPITE ANY PREVIOUS CLAIMS I HAVE MADE to the contrary, I have actual friends all over this country. All over the world! That way, I know I am loved in several time zones, but I don't have local people infringing on my free time for frivolous activities like "birthday parties" and "driving you to the airport" and "being there for you when you need emotional support."

All the maintenance required for friendships abroad is the biannual phone call or email. For those, you don't have to put on going-out clothes or find parking downtown—you can sit at home in your scuzziest pajamas and decide partway through the process to wear no clothes at all. This is extra true when you don't use FaceTime.

Essentially, long-distance friendships enable me to enjoy all the benefits of being alone without any of the crippling drawbacks of loneliness. It's a perfect setup—or so I thought.

You see, everything has a cost. The cost of my friendship strategy is that correspondence takes time. And I always have something else to do with my time. Things like, saving the nation from runaway fascism. I've started to suspect that, by gum, I am the one person on this earth with the smarts, the looks, and the God-given destiny to stop the insanity happening so fast that no single individual can keep up with all of it.

I mean, I see all kinds of ways out of this. I just need Congress to listen to me, and the state governors, and the National Guard, and NASA, and an assortment of woodland creatures. I'd have the whole kerfuffle dusted by Valentine's Day. If not this year's Valentine's Day, then certainly some year's.

But then I decide to read the internet. That's when I get downhearted. Immigration bans and administrative purges and healthcare defunding might just be shiny head fakes designed to distract us plebes from the actual shifts in power structure that will ultimately send us spiraling into a world where we'd consider cannibalism a reasonable alternative to swallowing this much doodoo.

Taking on the new world order makes me tired. So I take lots of naps. And when I wake up to discover that nothing has changed for the better, that makes me really, really, really want to talk to my friends. Except that I know we'll just end up rehashing the latest madness. And like I said, I have lots of other things to do with my time. Like writing Christmas thank-you notes.

These glittery, wintry cards have been sitting in their original packaging on my coffee table since December. And not the most recent December, either. You may be thinking that I should just pick up the phone and call my friends and family to say thanks. Maybe have an actual conversation while we're at it. But why do that when I can send them a card? A card is a tangible representation of my affection. A card also says, "Hey, friend and/or family member, you are special enough that I don't want our conversations to be traceable in any way."

That's right: in these recent times, I have become a paranoid survivalist. I don't want the government tracking any of my activities, even if it's just me thanking my grandparents for sending me a check instead of socks. I don't want the feds knowing where I shop, where I hike, who I talk to, or how much time, exactly, I spend reading listicles instead of working.

Basically, I am taking preemptive action here. The only way to stay entirely safe is to cease to exist. I mean, crazed fans aren't lining up to assassinate Meat Loaf, amirite?

But isn't that exactly what they want, the people you know who I'm talking about? To divide us, to isolate us? That's what will happen when we choose to live in fear and submission. And the antidote to division—isn't that connection?

Connection doesn't have to be on a large scale. Million-person marches. Grand demonstrations. It can also be two people who genuinely care about each other sending notes in the mail, calling each other just to say hi. Even if they end up discussing the Atwoodian dystopia at hand—isn't open communication precisely what brings us together?

So that's it. No more excuses. As an act of compassion and resistance, I'm going to call my friends. Right away. No stalling for nothing. I mean it. As soon as I figure how to tie off this section.

Guest Accommodations

I LOVE PEOPLE. Wonderful people do wonderful things all the time in this wonderful world of ours. Take Louis Pasteur. The work of that brilliant man means I can consume foods without dying from dysentery. In a world without people, I would stare into the refrigerator at night, wondering what bacteria-laden liquid to risk pouring over my raisin bran, and also wondering how I got a fridge in a world without people.

Which is to say, I am thankful for people. Each one has a part to play in this grand experiment we call Civilization. And they should stay there instead of coming to visit me in my own home.

Now I've had numerous people sleep on my couch, and I don't wish to single any one of them out. That's why I'll call them all "Tom," who crashed at my place this past weekend and got me counting once again the ways that houseguests dismantle my life.

For starters: I am obligated, as the host, to have food on hand. But I never know what Tom will want to eat. So I buy out the store's supply of bananas, so that I have some green, some yellow-green, some just past ripe, and some brown and slimy. A banana for every taste.

Also, having an impending houseguest requires me to do all my cleaning—of the entire house, mind you—in the same day. Even if it is not dirty by *my* standards, as the one who lives here and has to evade the mold in the dark. And even when Tom is a dude.

Why? Why do we force ourselves to tidy house for transient visitors more thoroughly than we ever will for ourselves? I suspect it has to do with our deep-seated need for acceptance. Either that, or we enjoy the righteous indignation when Tom drops his travel-worn possessions on our hastily wiped dining room table. It is a far superior feeling to the unjustified indignation we'd have were Tom's bags to improve the cleanliness of the table in its typical state.

So I've done all this cleaning in the hour after Tom texts to say he'll be here in forty-five minutes. And he doesn't acknowledge any of my efforts. Heck, he doesn't even seem to notice. I've dusted the entire kitchen area in hopes that the dog hair will stay on the floor, and the first thing Tom wants to do is go out to eat.

"Where's a good place to eat?" the Toms of the world like to ask, as if I know anyplace at all that isn't the rotisserie chicken by the grocery store checkout.

So we mosey to one of the two restaurants I can remember. There, I try my darndest to enjoy every bite and absorb the atmosphere. But that's really difficult when, the whole time, my mind is riddling out a puzzle unsolved since Egyptian times: Who is going to pick up the tab?

Normally when two guys dine out together, the bill is split. Separate checks, or two cards down the middle. But the rules change when one is an out-of-town visitor. I feel I ought to pick up the tab. After all, Tom drove all that way, and he is on vacation. Then again, Tom ought to pick up the tab, since I bought all those bananas.

What results is like an old dusty-street shootout. Two scruffy guys, staring each other down. Hands quivering over pockets. Waiting to see who draws first. Only here, he who draws first, loses. And then the shootout turns into a slap fight of "Oh, you sure?" "Yeah, I got it." "I should treat you." "Nah, I got this one." "Really?" "Really."

Day Two: rinse and repeat.

And the last thing about houseguests—this might be the worst thing of all—is that no fanfare feels appropriate to send them off when they finally leave. I offer Tom the bananas I bought as snacks for the road, and then he drives off, and then I realize how quiet the place is. How much I will miss my friend. And just when I feel my heart about to grow three sizes, I look around at the disheveled evidence of the whirlwind visit.

I could tidy it up. Or, you know what? It'll keep until next time.

Balking
the Walk

As a people, Americans have recently gone through one of the darkest periods in our history since forever. Our national nightmare began on an otherwise perfectly typical evening in early November 2016, when the impossible happened. Ever since, the darkness has had its unabated way with us through the coldest, shortest days of winter. But now, finally and inevitably, as it is every year, baseball is back.

Granted, baseball will never be the same again, not since the lovable cuddlable Cubbies won actual World Series games, elbowing out the Yankees and hoping none of us will notice the difference in pinstripes. But that little detail cannot much alter the euphoria that accompanies baseball in the air. Fresh clay, manicured grass, oiled mitts, hot dogs wrapped in hamburgers wrapped in bacon: these are the scents of spring.

In Colorado, of course, we have to imagine these smells, because spring does not happen here until autumn. But they exist somewhere, because spring training baseball is happening, and that means I can soon fulfill a long-neglected promise.

You see, there's this business associate of mine who claims she wants to learn to understand the game that is favored among America's elder populations. Or maybe she said she would never understand the game. Or maybe she said that baseball was boring. Or maybe it was golf.

Whatever she said, the mere possibility of a willing convert has me digging into the batter's box. And hey, if her claim is actually just a ruse to drink alcoholic beverages in front of an ESPN broadcast, then I still have the hope of a free beer in exchange for explaining ground rule doubles and intentional walks.

You may think this is a fool's errand. After all, not even umpires understand what a balk is. But I'm a persistent evangelist. The Mormons win you over with cheerfulness; I will win her over with endurance. There's 162 games a year, per team. That's 2,430 games each season, plus playoffs. Something exciting is bound to happen at least once! And even when it doesn't, every play offers a thrilling vocabulary lesson.

Take the intentional walk. It's the most so-called "boring" execution of strategy in the sport. When the fielding team (comprised of "fielders") decides it would rather put the batter (called "hey batter batter batter") on first base than give him the chance to hit the ball (called "the ball"), the pitcher throws four unhittable pitches (also called "balls") to the catcher, who "catches" them while standing far enough away from home plate to order a beverage from the vendor (called "hey, Beer Man!").

Nothing exciting ever happens during an intentional walk—except when it does. It turns out that professional athletes, who make hundreds of teachers' salaries by throwing and catching baseballs at high velocity, struggle mightily to throw and catch baseballs at normal human velocities.

This strange reality results in humorous bloopers, which people enjoy watching even more than Olympic-caliber excellence. And it adds tension to the simple act of playing catch, which is perhaps the most mundane recreation involving, conventionally, more than one person.

I mean, seriously. I spent half an hour just last night playing catch with my new dog. And Wally didn't even know how to play catch. I did not know this when I adopted him, but it would not have stopped me, because anyone can learn catch in no time. Catch is easy, yet mesmerizingly engrossing. I could charge people to watch Wally and me play catch, and they would pay. I could sell sponsorships. I could be a YouTube superstar. People say they watch baseball for the thrill of the home run, but let's be honest, they watch to see men play catch in matching outfits.

So imagine my disgust when I learned that the commissioner of Major League Baseball had deconstructed the essence of America's second- or third-favorite pastime, after football and working ourselves to the bone. He decreed that, starting this year, the intentional walk would require zero thrown pitches. The pitcher (who, nominally, is not a belly itcher) just says, "Yo, take your base," and that's that.

You can protest your congressional representatives and your fake news. Me, I'm taking a stand against the pitchless walk. If football still has to do kickoffs, and gymnasts still have to do floor routines, and we still bother to vote, then you cannot tell me that the intentional walk is pointless. It has a point. Namely, the point is that baseball is *full* of ridiculously specific customs.

In a sport with so much nuance, how am I ever supposed to explain the pitchless walk to my business associate? It's cheap and flimsy. The one facet of the game where no one has to do anything requiring any kernel of physical or strategic competence. Chewing Dubble Bubble and sunflower seeds at the same time requires more dexterity.

I'll never change my stance on this corruption of the sacred rules. But I will keep on talking about it, if it gets me out of explaining the infield fly rule.

Mullets and Other Tips for Success

I'D LIKE TO ANNOUNCE A WORLD DEBUT. This very book shall springboard a fantastic new idea which I myself just invented. Grip your seats, curl your toes, and prepare yourselves for: Throwback Thursday!

My editor tells me that Throwback Thursday, or #TBT to the cool kids, is already a "thing" in social media—or maybe she said it *was* a "thing"—where people post old photographs of themselves. The existence of this "original" Throwback Thursday could cause controversy for my own. But I'm not worried in the slightest. Just like Newton and that other guy who "invented" calculus, or Darwin and that other guy who "invented" evolution, history remembers the man with the better hair. Judging by my third-grade portrait with the quasi-mullet, I'm a shoo-in.

Besides, my #TBT tackles issues of more substance than embarrassing haircuts and ghastly clothes. To do so, it throws way far back. Back to when milk came in glass bottles and Coke's name hinted at its secret ingredient. Even farther, to when the biggest threat to civilization was Russia, that other time.

I throw us back to when the national news actually contained things like journalism. Investigative reporting. Context. You know ... *news*.

All we get anymore are people's opinions. We have pundits and experts and politicians, each one talking, writing, tweeting, posting, pinning, tumbling, threading, circling, and hashing, with very little actual reporting. In these times of everyone-has-an-opinion-so-why-not-broadcast-it, I'm as much an expert as anyone else. So my entirely valid diagnosis of the situation is that our society has more airspace and cyberspace to fill than ever before, but our attention spans are truncated by cat pictures.

The news these days must compete with that video your aunt posted of a cat with cancer, and if you don't share that video with all your friends in the next fifteen minutes, then your wishes won't come true and Bill Gates will eat a starving child. (Yes, the internet at times revives itself as one big chain email from the nineties, only deep fried in more conspiracies. Talk about throwbacks.)

Syrian conflicts and fatal spills of ethylene dibromide don't stand a Darwinian chance on the newsfeed. I mean, even I zoned out by the end of the word "Syrian," and I was writing it.

Instead of keeping the news succinct and digestible for us poor attention-deficient saps, news outlets opt to seize our attention with hyperbolic shenanigans that would shame a snake oil salesman. The news no longer matters because you wish to be an informed member of society. It matters only because Benghazi must boycott the Olympics or else Bill Gates will replace North Korea's launch software with Windows and we will all die.

With all this time and space to fill with opinions, seems to me that no one bothers to fact-check such claims. For starters, any fool on Google would realize that it's Steve Jobs' zombie corpse infecting North Korea's launch software with an incompatible version of iTunes Apple Music.

Besides, sharpening any idea to its most salient points is tough and time-consuming, and no one has time to hone ideas anymore. Mark Twain once apologized that he didn't have time to write a short letter, so he wrote a long one instead. What would he think of all these tweets ejaculated into the ether without even a proofread?

Spouting off in 140 characters doesn't make writing succinct; it makes it short. I know; I've tried tweeting to condense my writing. Turns out, it's not the size of what I say that matters, but how well I say it.

That's why my #TBT is all about giving our thoughts and words the time to crystallize. I gaze through my Throwback Telescope, and I spy an ancient time when brevity truly was the soul of wit.

I spy elementary school, when we first learned how to write haikus.

Haikus, you'll remember, are three-line poems with five syllables, seven, and five again. They distill a whole crop of ideas into a single flask of the finest thought-whiskey. No room for hyperbole here.

Let's try to write a haiku in the style of modern-day news shows, and see how it goes:

> What global warming?
> The government reads your brain!
> Bill Nye is a quack.

These opinions stand naked when written so succinctly, without all that white noise. They beg to be examined, to be questioned. They stimulate—gasp!—actual critical thoughts.

And the haiku accomplishes all that faster than posting a #TBT photo.

Crafting our words works as an automatic filter. When I have to distill my thoughts by actually thinking about them, I weigh every word and discard the scraps. Goodness knows you need some way to leash your tongue and get to the effing point already.

And that point is, you can't have a mullet if you let every hair grow wild. You have to trim back the business, so you can unleash the party.

Let us celebrate sharper, stronger thoughts! I toast this superior version of Throwback Thursday with one more haiku:

> Here's to brevity!
> May my editor stop me
> when I get long-win

Time Crunch

HAVE YOU NOTICED LATELY how everyone but me shows up an hour early? I mean, it's not like I was exactly competing for any Mr. Punctual awards before this phenomenon started. One of the perks of being a writer is that folks expect such eccentricities as me arriving late, or on a unicycle, or not at all. But this latest trend really had me wondering whether I was the sole punctual person in an Early World.

So I did some research. And, yes, I am the only conscientious person in America today, outside of Hawai'i and Arizona. We three entities stand united against the federally instituted rudeness that not only increases traffic accidents and heart attacks, and not only costs the economy $434 million a year, and not only forces me to lose an hour of sleep on Saturday night, but that also forces us all to lose forty *more* minutes of sleep on Sunday night, according to science.

No, not the Academy Awards. I'm talking about something much more sinister, if less controversial: Daylight Saving Time, the annual period where I forget whether it's "spring forward" or "spring back," because both make sense.

Daylight Saving Time has insinuated itself under the guise of "conserving energy." For instance, we conserve a ton of energy otherwise spent contemplating leaving our jobs. Just as it gets light outside in the mornings and we can see the beautiful world we're missing out on ... *BAM!* we're slammed back into predawn darkness. "Might as well go to work!" we whistle.

Also, we supposedly save electricity by not using lights during summer evenings. But studies show that these energy savings are more than offset by our air conditioners, except for those of us who don't have air conditioners, which fact drives us from our homes during the warmer months, which is why I go other places, where everyone else is an hour early. I am snagged in what the Germans call a *Teufelskreis*.

Yet despite snaring me in an ominous foreign word, "they" keep trying to sell Daylight Saving Time. "They" suggest that depriving us of just one measly little sleepy-time hour a year will allow us to barbecue with our families in that small window between work and binge-rewatching *Game of Thrones*.

However, when one peels back the layers, one discovers that Daylight Saving Time is not the real villain here. It's just the easy culprit to finger, like blaming laziness for obesity, or President Obama for World War I.

The real problem, clearly, is work. Going to work in the dark, coming home from work in the dark. It's work that keeps us from finishing our taxes, organizing the silverware drawer, and getting to know our children. I move we abolish work!

Of course, we can't abolish *everyone's* work. We have to preserve some essential jobs, like farmers, truck drivers, grocers, cooks, cleaners, street sweepers, street pavers, street painters, street walkers, the folks who make socks, pilots, garbage collectors, plumbers, publishers, tech support, doctors, and underwear models. But the rest of us will never have to worry about Daylight Saving Time—or clocks in general—ever again.

I realize that I am a dreamer, and my vision of utopia is unlikely to reach fruition so long as the underwear models' union maintains a death grip on democracy. So I propose a grand compromise: why don't we trade Daylight Saving Time for a shorter work week?

Hear me out. I, as a representative cross-section of middle-class white male America, have held a number of jobs wherein I spent the vast majority of my time pretending to look busy in order to remain on the payroll. My bosses believed that my tasks required eight hours a day, and my primary duty was to prove them right. In reality, they paid me to read web comics.

But humans are like gasses; we will fill whatever space is given to us. If my jobs had paid me just as much money, but given me only two hours to complete my tasks, I would have accomplished the same amount of work, while reading web comics much more hastily.

So if we all worked even four hours a day really, really hard, we could go home and barbecue to our hearts' content. We could all learn another language, and start riding unicycles, and show up late everywhere we go. We might even discover we like our families! Then my utopic vision would have to stick, because we'd all be completely unemployable.

Tax Bases

AMERICA'S MOST FAMOUS HOLIDAY is nearly here! But no need to panic. With two whole weeks until Tax Day, you still have a dozen restless nights before self-appointed experts slam you with opinion columns like "How to Make Past Years' Charitable Donations Today," "Smuggle Yourself to an Offshore Tax Shelter with These Perfectly Legal Steps," and "What If My Extension Lasts Longer Than Four Hours?"

I will have you know that I am different. I have never ordained myself an expert—that label adheres all by itself to geniuses (like me) who invent brilliant ideas (such as mine) for not paying taxes.

Before I spill the magic beans on legitimate tax evasion, you must promise to absolve yourself of any cloying sense of duty to your community. You may feel that your tax dollars are hard at work paving roads, managing sewage, feeding your neighbors in their times of hardship, and housing Belgians in *OUR* International Space Station. Such feelings of patriotic contribution are tough to diminish.

But to prove that your personal tax dollars make no difference whatsoever, I offer this litmus test: Without your wind beneath its wings, will the space station tumble from orbit, sparing any crushed bystanders from hearing another Nickelback song ever again?

Answer: Probably not, because I for one have never been so lucky.

Face it. Your taxes will not directly contribute to the common good. So you should find the most patriotic path to legitimate tax write-offs. And nothing is more American than saving yourself taxes at a baseball game.

That's right—you can spend an hour's wages on a hobbit-sized cinnamon twist and consequently fork over less money to Uncle Sam, the bum.

To cement your trust in my wizardry, let's take a look at

TAX DEDUCTIONS AT PLAY

Your favorite author travels to Arizona for surely legitimate business purposes, even if those purposes are too intrinsic to the ethereality of journalism to document properly. He buys tickets to a spring training baseball game. With what money is left after convenience surcharges, he buys food for tailgating, souvenirs for his future self, and a single lemonade. Over a dinner scavenged from ballpark trash cans, the columnist discusses legitimate business integration tactics.

> **Quiz:** What part of this trip is tax deductible?
> *(Hint: it's not the business dinner. The columnist forgot to scavenge any itemized receipts, and the IRS does not assign a monetary value to botulism.)*
>
> **Answer:** Every single other expense is tax deductible. *The critical clue here is often overlooked—your favorite author is a writer. Writing is his job! And he cannot be taxed on money spent for work-related outlays.*

So he writes a segment of a book incorporating the specifics of his recreational expenses. To wit: "I learned a great deal about respect by collecting autographs with a package of blue Bic pens and two Official Major League Baseballs from a box of twelve. That life lesson happened directly because the Royals' minor league players squeaked past the Reds' minor league players 3-2. I'm glad I ate lunch beforehand, because the lemonade cost approximately the second baseman's salary. Seriously, I have spied on third dates more affordable than that lemonade."

Now that these expenses are integral to a published chapter, your favorite author may deduct them from the applicable year's income.

THIS CONCLUDES TAX DEDUCTIONS AT PLAY

Folks, that's as simple as it sounds! And the Internal Revenue Code of the United States probably does not restrict or qualify this financial benefit in any way.

Of course, a puritanical work ethic is not the only way to earn tax write-offs. Retirement planning is another. I began hedging for retirement at the usual age (eight) when I purchased the first of many packs of baseball cards.

This retirement strategy works almost precisely like buying mint-condition action figures, or a house:

- Prevent the investment from catching fire for several years;
- Set the inevitable hoards of desperate buyers at each other's throats;
- Sell the investment at lemonade-level markups;
- Add the word "magnate" to your name plate.

I see no way in which such a simple plan could possibly ever fail me, unless, of course, everyone else also bought beaucoup baseball cards, at first inflating prices artificially and then bursting the bubble, leaving us long-term investors holding a bunch of expensive bookmarks.

No way that's already happened! And since I jumped on this investment train so far ahead of the curve that I personally have more Ken Griffey, Jr., rookie cards than I do social acquaintances, I should be set for a lifetime of financial freedom with no regrets.

Although, if I had the chance to do it all over again, I would advise eight-year-old me to stash his cash. He'll need it, once he's old enough to file extensions with the proper authorities.

College Apps

AS YOU HIGH SCHOOL SENIORPEOPLE, including my youngest sister, ride out senioritis until it crashes you on the shores of your freshpeople college semester, there's something you should know. Your parents (and other people who "just don't get it") may fail to treat you like the adults you are.

I get it. You have dreams, and you are going to change the world! You are spreading your fledgling wings, like young hawks coasting on a stiff nor'easter and tens of thousands of borrowed federal dollars. Yet the older adults in your life keep nagging. I recommend that you put up with them as best you can, because they have tender, loving reasons for their hovering, pestering behavior: they don't trust you.

But this isn't their fault! So-called "science" has brainwashed them into thinking that the impulse control function in your brains is not yet fully operational. They believe that your addled mind will coax you into risky behaviors, such as transforming the campus fountain into a Jell-O mixer or, much worse, majoring in philosophy.

For once, both "science" and your parents are absolutely right. Your brains are indeed a game of pick-up sticks played with cooked spaghetti.

This is a good thing! Your brains will never again be as flexible as they are right this moment. Use that ol' tangle of noodles to Find Yourself. Branch out from the family tree. Escape your parents' failed dreams and skedaddle out from under the shadow of your admittedly exceptional older brother.

As an unlicensed journalist who writes books anyway, I can vouch that college isn't about an "education" or a "career." It's about doing whatever you want for four—or, increasingly, eleven—of the most vibrant years of your life. For the first time since middle school, you will be free from the social pressures of high school, unless of course you join a fraternity, sorority, or other gang. Forge your own paths, soon-to-be freshfolks!

If forging your own anything intimidates you, take a page from my own personal playbook. I imagine one incident in particular is still envied across my alma mater: We Throw Rocks at Each Other for Fun, Officer. And that's not to mention the wild ride known as Trying To Flush a Full Garbage Bag Down the Toilet, nor the thrill-seeking adventure of Getting a B+ in Heidegger.

Granted, we did not have smartphones in my day. So if you want to have such guaranteed fun without it being held against you by the National Security Agency and/or your grandparents, you will have to download a time-machine app and travel to an era when "social media" meant a three-way phone call.

What I mean to say is, I do not personally know how difficult it is to untag myself in a photograph depicting someone—*not* me, probably—wearing a toilet seat like an Elizabethan collar. You freshbodies must navigate those waters on your own. But I do know another thing, which is that certain college activities are universal and timeless.

Ah yes. Freshdudettess and freshdudes, prepare yourselves for simpler and messier, if more reliable, college pastimes. These activities open the horizons of the mind, shatter conservative notions of intimacy, and set the foundations for a lifetime of sensory exploration.

I'm talking, of course, about eating at the dining hall.

Any freshhuman knows that a ten-dollar-a-plate buffet will never taste as delicious as free pizza. With this basic comprehension of the frugality-to-yummy ratio, you already understand more about economics than anyone in the federal government. Yet schools have to pay for football coaches' salaries *somehow*, which is why admissions advisors hornswaggle parents into signing you up for forty-two meals per week at the campus dining hall. Sure enough, after your first taste of "Mexican Monday," you will return only when you need leftovers with which to build the final project for your modern art course.

Believe it or not, college freshindividuals are not the only people coping with transitional periods right now. For instance, Congress may or may not be in an unfamiliar phase called "in session," when its members must—this is an untested theory—locate their own seats inside the Capitol building.

Others are going through more severe traumas, yet making much less fuss in the realm of lawn signs. These people are parents, guardians, and other former caretakers of college students. As they see it, their babies are just entering the Big Cruel World, and the Big Cruel World is rife with other people's much less perfect children.

To these folks, I'd like to offer a word of comfort: Well before going to college, your babies have already "been there and done that," whatever extracurricular "that" you most dread. Only now, they don't have to sneak behind your back! I find that to be a refreshing thought.

Besides, you can trust your babies to survive in the wild. They're smart; they've already installed every app for finding free pizza.

Out to Pasture

THE IRON HORSE BICYCLE CLASSIC has been happening for half a century. Wordplay! because it is a fifty-ish-mile ride, taking place for fifty-ish consecutive years. That's a lot of years of crazy people riding bicycles up mountains, haughtily disregarding Henry Ford's Promethean gift of motorized vehicular travel.

Riding in the Iron Horse is a noble feat. Yet I have to admit that my enthusiasm for the ride lost its tread this year.

That's because, in my five years participating, nothing has changed to make the event more challenging. The mountain passes are no higher than ever before. The road from Durango to Silverton grows no longer, and I am increasingly capable of not bothering to clean my bike's chain.

The only thing that changes are the bicycles themselves. These road bikes shed ounces every model year, to the point where a fully outfitted machine weighs as much as my threadbare underwear and a half a pair of socks. The idea here is that a lighter bicycle improves performance: less mass in the carbon frame decreases the time it takes for people to amass excessive debt.

My bike, however, does not change. It remains intact every year. Works for me, because having a reliable bicycle is the first necessity for riding the Iron Horse, along with bike shorts, bike shoes, bike cleats, bike gloves, bike jersey, bike helmet, bike sunglasses, Chamois Butt'r, and nothing better to do.

I have all those things in hand. Even so, I considered putting this year's Iron Horse out to pasture, except that I had already registered, and I couldn't use my commemorative water bottle in public if I did not ride for realsies on the big day.

The ride itself was not going to up the ante for me. I needed to switch things up myself. I needed some vigor in my regimen. Some enthusiasm. Some fresh perspectives, guaranteed to benefit me with wisdom, experience, and compulsory participation. So I entrusted my training to a pack of college kids.

Now it is probably unfair of me to call them "kids." After all, these college students were burgeoning adults, old enough at the time to have survived Y2K even if they weren't allowed to stay up til midnight for it. They were old enough to remember wondering what a VHS is, and to call Pearl Jam "classic rock," and to reminisce about getting their first iPhones in fifth grade. They were absolutely, unquestionably, barely qualified to give their elders exercise advice.

But I accepted their assistance gladly, because it would be different than accepting my own advice for the fifth year in a row.

Here's how it happened: I agreed to work with a team of Exercise Testing and Prescription students at Fort Lewis College, wherein one student would do all the work and the other four would sign their names to it. I volunteered my time and my body when the program was pitched with phrases like "taking into consideration your own personal goals" and "time commitment of about 2-6 hours."

Even I, with my bald-tired enthusiasm, could commit to two-to-six hours of Iron Horse training. Especially when one of those hours was utilized by filling out some high-intensity paperwork.

These students had all kinds of questions for me. What was my fitness goal this semester? (Finish the Iron Horse with minimal effort.) What health considerations should they take into account? (Do not ask me to change my diet if you value your own health considerations.) How active was I currently? (At the moment? Vigorously completing paperwork.)

The students collected my answers and said they would prepare a training regimen for me. I was ready for anything. But I was not ready when they told me I should aim to ride for eight hours—*every week*.

The students explained to me that the two-to-six range was for actual in-person meetings, where they would measure my height and pinch my armpit fat and count how many pullups I could do in a minute, even when it was very quickly evident that number would be zero. In order to meet my fitness goals, I needed to put in plenty of unsupervised hours.

I knew, in my heart, that they were right. Anything worth accomplishing is worth putting in time and effort and Gatorade. So I sucked it up. For the good of Education, and to show these younglings what we old farts are made of, I lied about my riding schedule.

Hey, I had to! I don't have eight spare hours a week. But I did ride, every week, at least once. And as the snow melted, my enthusiasm started to sprout alongside the aspen trees. I rekindled the pure joy of riding a bike, breathing the fresh mountain air, watching crows and hawks circle the skies. This is why I ride the Iron Horse. Because these blissful moments never change from year to year. As William Wallace said in 1995, "Every man dies; not every man really lives." Forget my ride times and my dirty chain. I was really living.

And then I really cried, because even *Braveheart* is now old enough to have kids in college.

Bootleggers Anonymous

I NEVER IMAGINED THAT LISTENING TO MUSIC would harden me into a criminal. But here I am, a renegade pirate sailing an outlaw ship on a wave of sound, striking fear into the hearts of strained metaphors everywhere. For I am now, unofficially and illegitimately, a bootlegger.

To keep the feds off my back, I won't go into details except to tell you that I recorded full audio from two consecutive Neil Young + Promise of the Real shows in Telluride. From the pit, just left of center stage, on a recording application cleverly concealed within a smartphone.

Look, if it makes any difference to you, I didn't do it to get rich. Even if I sold the tape at ten bucks a head to everyone in the audience—which I totally did not attempt to do—I would still not recoup what I spent on a concert T-shirt.

So why did I do it? I did it to capture the experience of hearing Neil Effing Young's first shows in this legendary mountain town. I did it for the lifetime bragging rights. I did it because I enjoy listening to live music from state-of-the-art sound systems, only at home and in garbled facsimile. I did it for the only reason a pirate does anything, excepting doubloons or wenches or eyepatches or notoriety: because I didn't figure I would get busted.

About not getting busted: I didn't have much of a plan, or any plan at all. I had something better than a plan. I had flawless camouflage, guaranteed to raise me above suspicion. An invisibility cloak, of sorts: I had a plaid flannel shirt.

Between my disguise and the all-weekend wrist band I obtained on the down-low in exchange for redeeming an all-weekend ticket, getting into the venue and avoiding detection from The Man were the easy parts. But to record my first full-length bootlegs, I still had to overcome significant challenges. I'd say, at a rough estimate, I had about one significant challenge for every beer sold on the premises.

Now I am a bit of a relativist. I think there is no wrong way to enjoy a concert, so long as that enjoyment does not involve arriving after showtime and wedging your three beers into the already-quite-intimate space around those of us who waited in line for hours to earn our prime seats. To fight for these "seats," by which I mean "standing room so sardined that your back hurts before the opening number," you'd almost have to be the kind of person who pays a $125 cover to get drunk on ten-dollar beers.

However, one's magnanimity wears off when one is attempting to preserve history on a smartphone. When one is striving to perfect the art of bootlegging on one's first try, one is less enamored with screaming, yelling, jostling, catcalling, Freebirding, and getting pushed out of the way so you can buy three more beers since (spoiler alert!) you spilled your first three.

In regular concertgoing life, one doesn't remember the weeble who wobbled a beer on one's shoes, or the brah who picked a fight because "his buddy is up there somewhere" and one wouldn't let him cut through, even though one grew genuinely afraid of leaving the venue on an EMT's arm. But when one is bootlegging, one records every little peep from the audience, and one wants to remember Neil Young, dammit, not the way everyone else sounded during Neil Young.

The whole project was being shot to pieces before my very ears. My bootleg would not be a triumph of piracy and outlawyery. It would be a testament to the crowd, the plebes, the people who are not true "fans" because they don't enjoy a concert the exact same way I do.

Midway through the first show, Mr. Young pulled out the electric guitar and delved into an extended jam. The song was longer than some bands' entire reunion tours. The song ran longer than a typical TV series on Fox. The song was so long that I saw a man leave his wife in the pit, return with a beer, and successfully salvage his marriage. And the song was glorious. It harmonized me with the universe, resonated with the cores of the mountains on every side, and defied further figurative language. It was worth the price of admission, plus the T-shirt.

And it made me forget all about my bootleg. I was there, completely there, completely present, completely alive while the song lasted.

I listened to the recording after the show, and yeah, it sounds like I taped it with a tin can and a piece of string. But it makes me nostalgic for the show. In all the noises, I remember the alpenglow of the opening numbers, the awe of the epic jam, the guy next to me peeing on the ground. I'll hope for a live album of the music someday. For now, I have the awareness of having experienced that moment.

And one final note to the Recording Industry Association of America: you need not worry about anyone else ever hearing this tape. Somewhere in the middle, I started singing along.

My Little Wookiee

When I adopted a dog four months ago, I vowed to myself that not every future piece of writing would be about him, because I am a well-rounded individual with diverse other interests to write about. For starters: I love taking walks with my dog, going to the dog park, and snapping photographs for my in-progress art series, called Portraits of My Dog.

But, once in a great while, I feel entitled to write about Wally, which (to answer his #1 fan mail question) is definitively short for Wallace. Today, I'd like to address his #3 fan mail question.

First, though, I imagine you are wondering what sort of fan mail comes to a dog. Here's an example. Wally's #2 fan mail question concerns his breed. I don't understand why people even ask this question, because people are quite good at answering it for themselves. Folks who have known Wally for a time shorter than a TikTok always have an opinion about what kind of dog he is, and they are always wrong.

But that's not what the questioners want to hear. So to appease them, I have started saying that Wally is a cross between two random alien races from *Star Wars*. This answer makes actual sense to me, because I've lately realized that I talk to Wally exactly like Han Solo talks to Chewbacca. And it's really, really difficult for someone to rebut with, "I dunno, man. I think see more beagle than gundark."

If that dialogue doesn't stop the conversation, fan mail question #3 really does: "What happened to his nose?"

It is a great testament to Wally's overall friendliness that petters continue petting him when they see his muzzle. It's not that it's gross or anything. More like, it looks sunburned. Like a sunburn on top of road rash.

This condition doesn't seem to faze Wally one bit. No itching, no scratching, no griping. And its flare-ups are not tied to anything I can identify. They could be an allergic reaction to diving into lizard-populated sage bushes just as easily as to, say, answering the same three questions over and over.

I could always brush off the topic with bromides and banalities. Instead, I've used these instances as "teachable moments," wherein I hoped these strangers could teach me what was up with Wally's snout. Because I had no clue.

These everyday Joes failed to crowdsource my answer, though, so I recently took Wally to the actual vet. She took one look at him before suggesting I sit down. I don't remember what she said, because I didn't want to hear anything difficult. But the next appointment ended with her sending off little pieces of my dog for a biopsy.

The biopsist—who, I understand, makes a living completing conclusive biopsies—sent back inconclusive results. (The invoice, however, was explicitly conclusive.) So while we're waiting on a second (or rather, another first) opinion, we are treating symptoms. And until the animal scientists invent a definitive answer for me, I am choosing not to think negatively. Or, really, at all.

That's why I took the dude on that camping trip—his first, as far as I know.

(You know how a significant other will say, "Oh, I used to go boating all the time with my ex—erm, with my friends?"

And then the resulting pause gets awkward because you *know* you're not the first to plant a flag on this moon but that doesn't mean you want to see the bootprints of previous astronauts? It's the exact opposite with an adopted dog. Wally's got three to five years of life already—his age is another "inconclusive result"—but he keeps mum about them. Everything we do together is a first, at least for me.)

Now I could tell you the dramatic story about how a mystical desert creek cured Wally's nose, and more importantly how our grand adventure taught us to weather life's many turbulent travails with love and optimism. But I would be lying.

Really, we were just a man and his Wookiee-Rodian mutt out under the stars, forgetting all about biopsies and mysterious disorders, eating beans and dog treats, lighting stuff on fire, treeing chipmunks, getting lost, getting found, and getting far, far away. Out where a man is a man and a dog is a dog, and the post office doesn't forward fan mail. Everything there was as simple as it appeared to be. And that was good enough for us.

WALLY AND ZACH WILL RETURN.

DAVE BARRY, THE ACTUAL AND FOR REAL Pulitzer Prize-winning humor columnist, once called me his personal idol. (I am not making this up.) He wrote it in my copy of his book *Peter and the Starcatchers* at a train-wreck of a booksigning at Harrod's of London where I was the only attendee and the shop announced his co-author, Ridley Pearson, as the illustrator. I know he does not write this in everyone's book because, in the copy I bought for my friend Andy, he wrote "Arr." Back in the day, Andy and I spent senior Honors English in the back of the classroom, dressed like hobbits and reading Mr. Barry's syndicated columns. If not for him—Mr. Barry, but also Andy, probably—this book would not exist, because I never would have figured out on my own that cracking long-form jokes in the newspaper was even an option. I wanted to put

"My personal idol." **– Dave Barry**

on the cover of this book, but my sister's husband's aunt's legal counsel advised that I not, without his express written permission. Even though saying so in the acknowledgments

243

will not help sell books, I am honored to be Mr. Barry's idol, and I sincerely hope he does not pursue any legal action.

I would like to thank some other people who were more directly involved in the creation of this book. My column, which I call "Fool's Gold" and my editors call "pushing deadline," has run in publications of higher quality than it deserves. Missy Votel with the *Durango Telegraph* gave me my start when, I suspect, she needed to fill out an Iron Horse issue on short notice. V. B. Price and Benito Aragon pushed me to go weekly for a time with the *New Mexico Mercury*. Gail Binkly with the *Four Corners Free Press* believed in the column enough to submit it for awards, some of which it won without any bribes heretofore known to me. And once Chris Kamler picked me up with the *KC Post*, I was able to say I was published on both sides of the Mississippi, even though that was factually untrue. Most every piece in this book ran originally in one or several of these fine outlets, only most of which are now defunct.

My dog Wally shacked up with me in an Airbnb while I took those columns and attempted to make a book out of them. My other dog Hawkeye got me to throw the ball for him when I needed a break from revising it three years later, and again (with his new brother, Ryzhik) three years after that. And while my dogs are the best dogs ever yes they are, they are still learning to read, so I must thank my best manuscript readers, including Magdalena Lily McCarson (with props for the author photo) and Hayley Kirkman (with props for the cover design). I appreciate your feedback and support along the home stretch. Also, I must thank both of my general readers: Mom (who always told me I could do this, and in ways beyond what moms are simply supposed to say, so I know she meant it) and Pops himself (with props for passing the paternity test). Some of these readers—let's call them "Pops" because that is his name—thought I should cut the section about Monster Skunk farting everyone to death. No offense, Pops, but this is why you are an engineer and I am not.

I also want to thank Jenny Mason, who read a great very many of these pieces in draft form and spared both of my general readers from some very poorly executed jokes.

I cannot thank my agent, because I do not have one. Every agent I queried rejected this book without reading it. Let this serve as inspiration to all aspiring authors out there: you, too, can keep the royalties from all seventeen copies of your book all to yourself. Which is why I'd like to thank you, yes you, you holding this book right now, which therefore makes you one of my dearest readers and living proof that dreams do come true. I mean, you or someone probably paid real money for this book, when literary agents wouldn't even read it for free. For that, I am grateful.

Speaking of paying real money for this book, I must thank the backers of its Kickstarter campaign, because we promised them inclusion in these Acknowledgments. So, from the bottom of my heart, I'd like to thank: Alison, Amaris Feland Ketcham, Andrew Goodin, the cosmically privileged Ava Burgos, Backer Buddy (aka William "Hoops" Grimes), the Bog Witch of Argo Dun, Buddy the beagle, Brandy Gaskins, Brynn Esterly, Carol & Brian Bondy, Clara Muriel Wetmore (because that is her name), Craig Hurd-McKenney, Deirdre, Diana Miller, Dr. Diane, Elizabeth Auden, Grace Darling, Hayley Kirkman, Jennifer Brown, Jennifer P., Jessica Stanley, Jo Douglas, Joanna Stingray, Jonatha Kottler, Karen Chrappa, Karen Stone, Keena Kimmel, Lani, Leslie A. Donovan, Lisa M. Polen, Liz & Yannick Vanhove, Mags, Merckx & Scooty Boots, Mia Brink, Michael C. Krauss, Miriam Rachel, Mom :0), Pamela G. Hively, Platon Karpov, Randy Watkins, Richard Spera, River Stingray, Scott & Kara Nellos, Stephanie Ann, and all of those backers who never completed their backer surveys. There. Now we're even.

I am also grateful for the people at Casa Urraca Press for making this book a reality. I cannot imagine a better publishing team, and not only because I have no other publishing team to compare them to. I would also like to thank every indie bookstore out there, and every bookseller. You all make the world a better place, whether or not you feature this book on your curated lists and your prominent display tables.

And last but not least, I would like to thank Sugar, who—Wait. I never finished Sugar's story with the flies and Kevin Spacey! I *swear* I'll finish it in the next book.

ZACH HIVELY AND HIS DOGS live in northern New Mexico. He continues to write and (somehow) publish the long-running *Fool's Gold* column, which has (somehow) won several first-place awards from the Society of Professional Journalists' Top of the Rockies awards. He has written three books of poetry so far, including *Owl Poems* and *Wild Expectations*. His *Desert Apocrypha* earned the Reading the West Book Award for poetry. Lest you try to find him in person, be warned: he plays the harmonica but refuses to get better at it.

You can learn more about his work at zachhively.com. You can also read frequent new work, plus receive updates on writing workshops and forthcoming publications, by subscribing to *Zach Hively and Other Mishaps* on Substack.

CASA URRACA PRESS publishes creative works by authors we believe in. New Mexico and the U.S. Southwest are rich in creative and literary talent, and the rest of the world deserves to experience our perspectives. So we champion books that belong in the conversation—books with the power, compassion, and variety to bring very different people closer together.

We were founded in the high desert somewhere near Abiquiú, New Mexico. Visit us at casaurracapress.com to browse our books and to register for workshops with our authors.